THE THREE

GAPS

between
GOALS and GREATNESS

A Parable About Leadership Practice

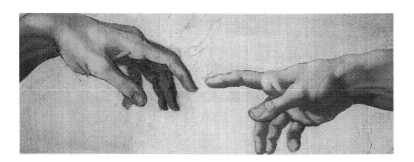

Pelè Raymond Ugboajah, PhD

Pelè Raymond Ugboajah, PhD

For Rekiyatu: my wife, soul mate, best friend, and greatest inspiration.
For my children: Ijeoma, Obinnamdi, and Ikennamefule.

Pelè Raymond Ugboajah, PhD

Contents

Pelè Raymond Ugboajah, PhD

Introduction

The biggest challenge organizations face is execution—otherwise known as *getting things done*. The reason? There is a natural chasm between the goals a leader sets and the results —or greatness—that is ultimately achieved by the people in his or her organization. In other words, most leaders realize that knowing what to do and actually getting it done through others are two completely different challenges. After years of studying and experiencing this phenomenon, I found that the most effective way to bridge the execution gap is to address it as several constituent gaps all working together, as opposed to thinking of it as one monolithic business challenge.

The more obvious set of gaps have to do with people achieving tangible results. You might call this set of gaps the *performance* side of the execution gap. These are things like organizational or job-specific goals and deliverables, which most companies generally make a fair attempt at measuring and monitoring through performance appraisals. However, there is another set of gaps that go largely unaddressed, despite the fact that most people will agree it is the proverbial elephant in the room. This second set of gaps— otherwise known as 'people issues'—comprises what I call the *behavior*, *habit*, and *community* gaps. These three gaps, albeit more intangible, have the undeniable power to either support or seriously undermine organizational success. No matter how much performance a leader demands from his or her people, success will only be possible to the extent that people's individual and community behaviors can be turned into positive organizational habits.

Here are the three gaps between goals and greatness:

Gap	Description
Behavior:	When leaders and employees don't measure, monitor and improve behavior goals alongside performance goals.
Habits:	When leaders and employees don't practice desired organizational behaviors until they become habits.
Community:	When leaders and employees don't form safe communities of practice where they can develop positive behavioral habits.

The three gaps between goals and greatness are exemplified in a phrase that goes like this: "She's a good nurse, but..." In the healthcare field, this phrase refers to that technically gifted and talented nurse whom everyone knows is excellent at performance, but struggles on the behavioral side. Of course, the phenomenon is not unique to healthcare, and you may have heard a phrase like that before in other industries: "He or she is a good (fill in the profession here) ... BUT ... their behavior sucks!" We've all heard of that talented leader or employee who is good at their job, but struggles when it comes to interpersonal communication, relationships, leadership, or teamwork. They bring others down, and frequently frustrate important projects. However, despite their behavior, they are tolerated and sometimes even thrive in organizations if they possess enough political clout.

In any industry, the behavior, habit, and community gaps constitute an insidious and devastating problem because they creep in and gradually undermine the well-made plans of an organization or team, despite everyone's best intentions. The result is usually lowered employee morale, dysfunctional teams, and bad customer service. Sometimes, the consequences are more severe, such as in the healthcare field where patients' lives are at risk, or, as you'll see in this book, in the case of Enron, where it was behavior—not performance—that brought down a major multinational corporation, and negatively impacted the entire US economy.

What should be done when so many leaders and employees may be good technically, but struggle behaviorally, thus creating or worsening team and organizational dysfunction? Unfortunately, what most organizations do is either ignore these people, or fire them. There is rarely a robust solution in the middle, and therein lies the real problem! If you do nothing, you get continued dysfunction in teams and continued potential for negative organizational outcomes. If you simply wave a wand and fire people, you might be prematurely getting rid of talented, well-meaning employees in a business environment where talent is scarce. What other option is there?

Thankfully, a third option exists, and it lies in vigorous leadership and workforce development. However, far too many of today's leadership development methods are ineffective, stuffy, boring, and overly focused on discovering what's wrong with people psychologically, as opposed to advancing what's right and potentially great about them. But it doesn't have to remain that way. This book will show that development can be much more positive, effective, and even fun, when people learn to *practice* leadership the way you might practice sports or music.

Pelè Raymond Ugboajah, PhD

> Everything is practice! —Pelè of Brazil

Consider for a moment, one of the most common debates on the topic of leadership training: the question of *nature versus nurture*. One school of thought holds that leadership is a set of innate, natural traits that some people are born with. The other school asserts that leadership is a set of skills that people can learn. This book is written from the viewpoint that truth can be found on both sides, although I favor the argument that we all have leadership potential within us, and that potential can be developed and improved through learning. The question becomes: how can we develop leaders in ways that are positive and engaging, not boring and stale? I want to help you see leadership development through completely different lenses.

Leadership is like playing a piano or soccer or giving a speech or skydiving from ten thousand feet. Leadership can be fun, exhilarating, and exciting. But most of all, leadership is a skill that can only be attained and perfected through *practice*, which is an inherently exciting and engaging process. Yes, for some people, leadership starts from a set of inherited traits, and for others it can indeed be learned; but for anyone who wants to take his or her leadership to the next level, leadership skills and behaviors *must* be practiced!

I wrote this book partially because, like the 'good' nurse, I've personally suffered while serving in various corporate leadership positions, not because I lacked performance skills, but rather because of behavioral and political struggles in team environments. It got so bad at one point, that the politics of working in corporations literally sucked the wind out of my personal passion

The Three Gaps between Goals and Greatness

for leadership. I found myself consistently discovering that every leader I knew was simply winging it when it came to leadership. Leadership for them was a matter of innate traits such as political acuity, charisma, or good speaking skills. No one used a structured process for practicing (and therefore, improving) the many fundamental leadership skills and behaviors we know of, the way a star athlete or musician might do for the essential skills in their professions.

The great practice-related attributes—the repetition, the devotion, the daily passion, and the community of feedback—that you might find in sports or music performances were completely absent. In my corporate experience, you simply got a title presented to you, and the inevitable options were: *sink or swim*. I couldn't accept that, so I borrowed a leaf from my namesake, Pelè, and decided that I was going to learn to practice behavior and leadership as hard as he practiced soccer, or as hard as I had learned to practice my own unique talents: writing, speaking, and music. I soon found that through practice, I was able to improve my behavioral and leadership skills in the same way that I had been able to improve my abilities on the piano or win awards as a Toastmasters public speaking champion. Over time, I became very passionate about practice, and my goal with this book is to share that passion with the world.

This book is neither a traditional management text nor a standard novel. Rather it is a hybrid—a story I'm telling as much from my heart as my mind. Therefore, I've divided it into two main sections: a *parable* and a *point*. I believe that the parable you're about to read will highlight one of the significant and continuing challenges organizations face—the need to find effective ways to develop leaders. After you've read the parable, read the point that the parable makes; there you'll get a summary of the LeaderPractice process, as well as some *free* tools to help you quickly get started toward building an effective workforce that will bridge the execution gap in your organization. If you enjoy listening to music, check out the song at the end of the book: 'She's a Good Nurse, But…' and visit www.leaderpractice.com to download it for free!

Finally, this book is not about describing the three, five, or nine best steps to becoming a great leader. There are already countless books on that subject. Rather than rehashing leadership definitions or traits, this book is about helping you practice actionable leadership skills that will help you close the execution gap in your organization. Together, let's take the mystery and psychology-dominated stuffiness out of leadership development, and let's put the passion of practice into it! Everything—including leadership—gets better with practice!

Pele Raymond Ugboajah, PhD
The LeaderPractice Guy

The Three Gaps between Goals and Greatness

We are what we repeatedly do. Excellence, therefore, is not an act, but a habit. —Aristotle

Pelè Raymond Ugboajah, PhD

Pelè Raymond Ugboajah, PhD

Part 1: The Gaps

Pelè Raymond Ugboajah, PhD

The Three Gaps between Goals and Greatness

Prologue

SKILLING GETS 24 YEARS.

Ex-Enron CEO sentenced for his role in the grand-daddy of corporate frauds. By Shaheen Pasha, CNNMoney.com staff writer

October 24, 2006: 9:32 AM EDT

HOUSTON (CNNMoney.com) – Former Enron Chief Executive Jeffrey Skilling, who gained infamy as the man who orchestrated the largest corporate fraud in history, was sentenced to more than twenty-four years in jail Monday.

The fifty-two-year-old Skilling stood stoically, his hands clasped before him, as presiding Judge Sim Lake handed down his sentence. His wife, Rebecca, however, sobbed quietly in her seat as victims of Enron's collapse watched the proceedings stone faced.

Speaking to reporters outside of the courthouse, Skilling said he was disappointed by the judge's sentence but was hopeful that "if we review this in a calmer atmosphere," the appellate judges may find in his favor.

Skilling and his attorneys have maintained that he couldn't receive a fair trial in Houston, the epicenter of Enron's implosion. "I'm not happy about it, but I believe deep down—and this is not an act—I believe I am innocent," he asserted.

Pelè Raymond Ugboajah, PhD

The CEO

I hate to say this," Ravi Sharma said in a faint Indian accent, "but I told you so!" His face was twisted in the mischievous and rueful grin he used whenever he was on the verge of making a poignant observation. At first I thought he was about to make some self-serving, arrogant point about the hot news of the day: the impending collapse of our biggest client, Enron. I studied him as he simultaneously navigated the busy Houston traffic and adjusted his professor-style glasses higher up his long nose. His wise-looking, sixty-something Eastern features became fixed in a stern gaze as he stopped at a red light on the corner of Washington Avenue and Sawyer Street.

He spat out in a high-pitched voice, "LeaderTraits is done!"

I sat motionless in his passenger seat, running my eyes from the cold BMW 7-series dashboard to the streets outside. The towering skyscrapers of downtown Houston loomed high above us in the morning sky, like steel and glass giants growing reluctantly out of a grey, concrete wasteland.

"If we can't turn our company around," he said, "I'm not sure what I'll do."

He looked tired as he held the steering wheel. His large hands and thick fingers were in sharp contradiction to his well-spoken, executive manner. I often found myself wondering how a short, physically small man like Ravi possessed such a large presence.

To me, Ravi wasn't just the CEO of LeaderTraits. In my mind, he was a mentor and a leader's leader, even if he had to physically look upward at practically everyone he ever met.

"So, are you going to quit?" I surprised myself with my own bluntness.

"Now there's a smart idea!" Ravi said, rolling his eyes, with sarcasm written all over his face. "No. I've got to fight this thing one more time. LeaderTraits needs to realize once and for all that we can't remain in the personality-traits business forever. We've got to move away from merely analyzing the "people" problem for our clients and start being part of their solution."

"Ravi," I said, frowning and shaking my head. "Don't you think this is a dead-end battle? I mean, LeaderTraits has been focused on the personality assessment business for decades."

"I don't give a damn!" he barked. "We've got to start helping our clients bridge their execution gaps. If losing Enron isn't enough to turn us around, then nothing will."

He had a point there. LeaderTraits was a twenty-two-year-old leadership development firm that was started in the late eighties as an outsourced personnel assessment shop for Enron. The two industrial psychologists who founded the firm were originally partners in India, but they moved the firm to Houston, right next to the Enron Towers, as business boomed over the years. How could you change the viewpoint of ancient industrial psychologists that constantly reminded you that they had been successful doing things their way for years, long before your time? How could you win when the dominant culture of the firm was geared toward performing personality assessments for a few high-paying mega-clients, rather than toward achieving lasting behavioral change for them? The answer was simple: you couldn't win because money talks. Most of the money we made came from Enron and whatever assessment business they tossed at us.

"Mike," Ravi said, interrupting my rumination over the Enron collapse. "I want you to share your new presentation about leadership practice with the executive team this afternoon."

I was flattered. In the almost three years I had been at LeaderTraits, Ravi had always shown an interest in my professional potential. Just recently, he promoted me to the position of director of leadership development, and set me on a path for greater leadership responsibilities within the firm. Because of him, I had become more than just another research-focused management consultant and PhD at an industrial psychology firm. He had helped me see the importance of selling tangible value and developing leaders. And the title didn't hurt either. I was now Dr. Mike Jordan, director of leadership development.

However, despite what I felt was his professional appreciation of my work, Ravi had a way of sending mixed signals. For example, throughout our drive back to the office after that morning's sales call, he hadn't said a word about my presentation. I hadn't been sure if he actually liked my new theory for developing leaders or not, and now all of a sudden, he wanted me to present it to his executive team.

"Do you think they'll be in the mood for new ideas today?" I asked.

"They'd better be!" he said, with his legendary firmness. "New ideas are the only way we're going to grow. They need to hear some of the stats you quoted today, like the one about how companies are losing up to 40% in financial value because of their inability to get people to execute their goals. That was a great point!"

"My favorites," I said, joining his rant, "were the ones about how 95% of the workforce in most companies don't understand their organization's goals, and how 86% are simply not motivated."

"Exactly!" Ravi exclaimed. "My stuffy executive team needs to hear these things!"

Ravi's background wasn't in psychology. He was a sales guy at heart and was more concerned with results than academic details. After emigrating from India in the late 1980s, he had proven himself to be a star sales executive at some of America's most successful medical technology companies. After that, he went back to school and got a degree in hospital administration and then worked his way up through the medical administration ranks to do a four-year stint as the CEO of a for-profit Texas hospital. LeaderTraits had hired him about five years ago, precisely because of his street-smart, no-nonsense, sales and leadership talents. They had wanted someone who could come into the firm and help drive profits. It was a great fit because Ravi's main goal in business and life revolved around how to find and please customers. He held no strong allegiance to any of the academic theories that the rest of us PhDs liked to flaunt around the office, but he knew instinctively when something could be useful to him. I think he must have felt that my new presentation was exactly the kind of weapon he could use to try to crack the intransigence and impenetrable walls of LeaderTrait's assessment-loving PhDs.

"Look," he said, with a matter-of-fact look on his face. "We are in clear and present danger of collapsing, especially when Enron, our biggest assessment client, is gone. I have no problem with assessments—that's our cash cow—but we've got to start building business offerings that go beyond that. We've really got to go beyond helping businesses assess people and start helping to develop their people."

"Agreed," I said, but I felt like playing the devil's advocate. "Remember that parable you told me about great leaders? You said a great leader is someone who knows how to bring about change slowly without totally destroying a company's culture or firing everyone in sight."

"That's right," he said. "That was the parable about the dog who lost his real bone by greedily going after the bone's reflection. Good. You remember well, Mike. But I didn't tell you that in real life, subtle change will work sometimes, but when it doesn't, you've got to go after big change. And if that doesn't work, maybe we do need to quit."

I nodded in quiet acceptance as Ravi made the last turn onto Louisiana Street. He always had a way of bringing his parables of wisdom into our conversations. We parked in the Clay garage, just a block north of the Enron Tower. As we made our way through the lobby, up the elevators, and finally to our forty-second floor office in the Wedge International Tower, Ravi walked like a man on a mission, marching into the next war zone. Despite his sometimes-abrasive style, he was nonetheless easy to admire. I wondered if this would be my last opportunity to work with such a wise, determined leader.

Pelè Raymond Ugboajah, PhD

LeaderTraits

"Baxter's dead," said Deepak, calling the executive team meeting to order. "They think it was a suicide." Deepak Amar was ancient, literally and figuratively. He never minced his words or cut corners. He had earned his PhD in organizational psychology from Harvard back in the late seventies, and was the only living founder of LeaderTraits. Back when they started the firm in the late eighties, most of the attention in the field was being paid to character traits. The firm was a breakaway success back then, helping large organizations select and assess executives for key leadership positions. Today, with forty-two executive consultants and supporting staff, Deepak was proud that LeaderTraits had come all the way from its humble roots in India to become a well-known U.S. industrial psychology firm. But today, standing tall and lanky, there was a hint of desperation in his voice.

"No one is returning my calls at Enron," he said, sitting down. "I think all hell is breaking loose over there. We need a survival plan."

Ravi cleared his throat and jumped in, eager to make the point he had been harboring all morning. Ignoring the news about Enron, he launched into the ramifications for LeaderTraits.

"I think this is one of those watershed moments when we need to reassess our core strategies." All six heads around the table turned toward him. He was sitting in his usual spot, strategically at the head of the table. Behind him was an entire wall made of glass, which featured a breathtaking view of Houston's central business district. The high afternoon sun shone through the glass wall and bounced off of Ravi's oversized chair. He looked diminutive, sitting in his big chair, calmly poised, as though his weapons were at-the-ready for a showdown.

"I think that for too long," he said, "we've let our clients like Enron use us as an assessment body shop. But the real value of what we can do as a firm has not fully been revealed to them." He looked around the room, as if to see who would be the first to oppose him, and sure enough, Abigail Kapoor chimed in. She was the most celebrated industrial psychologist in the firm. She was very proud of the many important leadership assessments she had conducted for clients over the years. Dark-haired and almost regal in her demeanor, she had married into one of India's wealthiest business families. Even more powerful than Deepak, she was the real influence peddler at LeaderTraits.

"Ravi, we've had this discussion before," Abigail said. "At this point, we now know for sure that Enron is going down. Don't you think we ought to be in damage-control mode right now?"

"No, actually, I don't," quipped Ravi, his rueful grin lighting up again. "I think it's time for something more like total-reset mode. Now we can all see in action what some of us have been warning would happen if one of our top clients pulled out. If what we hear on the news is true, today alone, we have already lost about ten million dollars from this year's forecasted income." Ravi made a fist with his right hand and pounded it ever so lightly on the table. "Folks, this is why we need to diversify our client base and change our core go-to-market strategy. Basically, we're going to have to remake this company."

The Three Gaps between Goals and Greatness

You could cut the silence in the room with a knife. Ravi had shown that over six years he could deliver on slow, incremental progress on the bottom line, but never had he been so blunt about demanding this much change all at once. And never had he done it with all of the most powerful members of the organization present at the same time. He made eye contact with every single person in the room, and then continued.

"I've brought Mike in for this meeting. I want him to share a new service strategy that we ought to consider. Not only do we need a new sales strategy, I think that we need to overhaul our entire service and delivery approach."

There was an uncomfortable silence in the room.

"Mike," Ravi announced, looking at me. "Can you please run through some of the thoughts you shared this morning at the Medtech sales call?"

I stood up, rattled and nervous, the way you might feel if someone told you your task was simple; just hold this bull here by the horn. Even though I had been with the firm now for almost four years, I had never fully become comfortable with Deepak and Abigail—the old guard—and I never felt fully accepted by them either. I cleared my throat.

"Thanks, Ravi," I said, respectfully, and then turned my gaze in Deepak's direction. "I think that we are focusing most of our service resources on leadership traits and not enough on creating lasting behavioral change within organizations. By focusing most of our energy on delivering psychological assessments, which are used as part of performance reviews, we are not doing enough to help our client organizations actually implement the kind of behavioral change that will help them meet their performance goals. Enron is just another tragic example of what can go wrong when the overriding focus of an organization is performance, while employee behavior is left to evolve unchecked."

Pelè Raymond Ugboajah, PhD

"Mike, we don't need to apologize for focusing on assessments," Abigail cut in sharply. "Assessing leadership traits is our business model. For goodness sakes, we are LeaderTraits! Are you saying that, indirectly, our core business model had something to do with Enron's collapse?"

"Yes, and no," I said, with a courageous lump in my throat. I walked over to the chalkboard. "May I make you a quick sketch?"

"Sure," Abigail said. I then proceeded to sketch the following diagram:

"I know you've all seen this iceberg analogy before, but please humor me while I use it to explain this particular point. Imagine that's the Titanic in the middle there. It's kind of like focusing on the visible, above-water part of an iceberg, while ignoring the under-water part that really causes the damage. Think of organizational performance as the visible part of that iceberg—it's the end result we all see. Now think of the invisible part of the iceberg, the part that's underwater, as employee and leadership behavior, which ultimately creates the performance output we see above the water. Organizations cultivate and measure performance often, but they seem to ignore behavior, which is ever present and responsible for the quality of their performance in the first place. That's the execution gap—failing to focus on the behavior side of the equation as much as the tangible performance side. It's like setting goals and unleashing employees in an almost Darwinian, behavioral free-market, where the strongest organizational politicians win, and the rest simply perish! I'm merely saying that our executive coaching engagements might seem nice on paper, but they are really not helping our clients mold the kind of lasting behavior and culture they need to be successful. And yes, I'm saying that, in today's business world, Enron is excellent proof of what happens when behavior—the unseen part of the iceberg—is ignored."

"Can you show us empirically what you're talking about?" It was Deepak. He loved scientific proof. "Otherwise, I'm not sure why we should be wasting precious time considering new approaches, especially when our proven practices have been successful for years."

"Here are some statistics," I said, handing out prints from our earlier sales presentation. "In a *Harvard Business Review* article, Mankins and Steele found that the execution gap can be responsible for up to a 40% loss in an organization's financial value. Now that's a tangible, clear, negative outcome that occurs when our clients allow behavior to go unaddressed."

Ravi jumped in to my defense. "What Mike is saying ought to be self-evident. It's one thing to help our clients reveal employee, team, or leadership flaws, but its another thing to help them fully implement the kind of lasting behavioral change that produces organizational results."

"So what exactly is wrong with our executive coaching processes?" Jim jumped in, with a puzzled, defensive look on his face. He was one of our most senior and respected executive coaches.

"Look at our clients," I said. "Most of the leaders we work with are just winging it everyday. They never put in any time to actually practice and improve their leadership. The problem with our executive coaching work is that we meet with those leaders far too infrequently, and then we send them off to improve their behaviors on their own, without any safe community of practice or support in their own context and environment. Enron was our biggest client, and all we did was give them psychological assessments on demand. We never really helped them do more than justify what they were already doing. Sure, we showed them what human capital skills and behaviors they needed, but nothing ever got executed. Nothing ever got done, and their culture remained the same—no, scratch that. It grew worse, as we can now see."

"So what's your solution?" Deepak asked.

"This morning, at Medtech, Ravi asked me to present a new, brain-based development approach for employees, teams, and leaders. It's a really straightforward concept, and it's all about setting up opportunities for intense, behavioral role-play and practice within organizations. I call it *LeaderPractice*, and it's essentially how companies can make the shift from great intentions to organizational greatness. It's the same basic methods that allow you to go from not knowing how to ride a bike, to riding one without thinking. It's the same methods that allow your fingers to magically *remember* the notes on a piano after you repeat a phrase over and over. And it's the same method that athletes use to turn skills into winning habits. If all these years, we had helped Enron grow positive habits within their workforce instead of just supporting their *rank or yank* approach, who knows if they'd be in this spot right now?"

Deepak and Abigail looked at each other without betraying any emotion on their faces. Ravi was studying all the faces on his team to gauge their responses. Most of the executive team members kept solid poker faces, and no one showed any response one way or the other to my cool little speech. Finally, Abigail broke the awkward silence.

"Mike, thanks for your work," she said. "I think we understand. Please leave us. We're going to continue this meeting in camera."

I thanked the executive team for their time and left the boardroom. However, something didn't seem right. I could feel it. Without looking into any of the open office doors in the hallway as I passed, and without making any eye contact with Kelly the office receptionist, I slid back to the relative safety and anonymity of my office.

Pelè Raymond Ugboajah, PhD

The Bush Rat and the Lizard

I grabbed some coffee and sat down to review my e-mails. In my inbox were several updates on the latest news at Enron. Baxter was indeed dead. They found his suicide note, and the entire leadership team at Enron was under close observation. The whole thing was uncanny. We had been just another vendor attending countless meetings with Enron employees, managers, and executives to decide how to help them with leadership assessments, team assessments, and employee performance appraisals. Throughout our process of working with them, we gave them prescriptive advice on what needed to be done to improve individual and team morale, performance, ethics, etc. We routinely ran their top leadership prospects through special role-plays and 360-degree psychological assessments. Heck, we even coached them on everything ranging from better executive presence to stronger business presentations. Throughout all these engagements, they gladly paid us our million-dollar fees but did pretty much nothing with our suggestions. So, whose fault was it? Was it theirs for not demanding that our work as consultants be held accountable against ethical, desired results? Or was it ours for gladly stuffing our pockets with their money, while turning a blind eye to whether or not they actually achieved lasting behavioral change? I didn't have any good answer.

Just then, Ravi walked in.

"It's over," he said.

"What's over?"

"I'm done," he said, shrugging his shoulders. "LeaderTraits and I have decided to part ways. It was a mutual decision."

I took a moment to let it all sink in. I hadn't seen this coming so fast, and the personal implications for me were gigantic. Ravi was not only my boss, but also, a cherished mentor. He was actually, dare I say, a friend. Ever since we met, I had felt as though he appreciated my talents, in part because I displayed more sales savvy than most of the other PhDs. For one thing, although I was in my forties, I was a recent graduate, and had been an entrepreneur for most of my career. Ravi used to always make the joke that, because of my background, I was probably the only PhD in the firm that didn't have my nose stuck up my ass. (That was his way of saying that I wasn't hung up on assessments as the end-all and be-all of our business.)

He sat down in my guest chair, his rueful grin absent.

"So," I asked him, "what will you do next?"

"I think I'll take some time off and figure out how to get back to my original plan."

"And what might that be?"

"To follow my bliss," he said, inspecting his nails. I liked that. It was typical Ravi wisdom.

"I think maybe I'll travel the world or do some public speaking. Heck, I might start by rejoining Toastmasters, or maybe even organize a jazz band." Ravi and I shared not only the same career field in leadership development, but also two creative hobbies we both were devoted to: music and public speaking.

"Those are great ideas," I said. "But what about work? Don't you plan to maybe start your own firm, or look for another CEO opportunity?"

The Three Gaps between Goals and Greatness

"No. I think I'll let that part of my life just relax for a while. I think I'm a little bit burnt out on management consulting at the moment. I am sick and tired of bumping into executives who shout at the top of their lungs that people are their greatest asset when all they truly care about are processes and performance results. And I'm sick and tired of industrial psychology firms that claim to be leadership development firms, when in fact, they never want to do more than performing psychological assessments."

"I couldn't agree more," I said, looking with bleak, vacant eyes out of my window at the Houston skyline.

Ravi brought my focus back to him. "You know what, Mike?"

"What?"

"This whole thing reminds me of the parable of the bush rat and the lizard."

"And which parable is that?" I asked, knowing that I was about to get another sampling of Ravi's unique brand of wisdom.

"There was once a bush rat, who badly wanted to find success in an organization full of lizards. The bush rat had great communication skills, great vision, and in fact, overall, he was a great leader. The only problem he had was that he was not a lizard, and unlike the lizards, he didn't have any strong desire to maintain the status quo. When he first joined the firm, all of the other executive lizards liked him, until he started to show his more outspoken and innovative side. All of a sudden, they started growing weary of his new ideas, which he kept introducing daily. One day, the executive lizards called him aside and warned him that if he didn't change and become more like a lizard, they would fire him. They wanted things in their organization to remain just as they had been for ages. But the bush rat resisted, and in his stubborn manner, he eventually accepted a challenge to a duel with one of the leading lizards. When the day of the duel arrived, a heavy storm began, and it was raining profusely. At first, the bush rat didn't understand why the lizards were all celebrating right before the fight, but it soon became obvious," Ravi said and paused for a moment.

"What happened next?" I asked.

"Nothing short of a disaster. The bush rat lost the fight in the rain, and to make matters worse, he drowned in a puddle of water right after the fight. You see, lizards are amphibious, and can survive in wet environments, but bush rats don't swim or dry very quickly because of all their fur. The unfortunate bush rat died because he didn't realize that he was trying to survive in the wrong environment. Like all the other leaders, he had received a psychological assessment that told him he was different, but no one ever gave him any leadership development tools to improve his chance for survival. So, naturally, he drowned in the rain of politics. That is why the saying goes: a bush rat should never fight in the rain with a lizard."

It sounded to me as though Ravi was talking about himself.

"So, are you the bush rat?" I asked.

"Yes," he said. "But so are you."

"How so?" I asked.

"Well, I think you're a bush rat because you actually care about implementing behavioral change, but you're trying to survive in a firm where no one could care less about that. You're trying to bring change and innovation, when all they want here is the same thing Enron wanted—high performance regardless of what behavior was used to achieve that end."

I nodded my head. Ravi's parable rang very true for me.

"I think that there are two kinds of leaders on this planet," he continued. "There are those bush rats like you and I who care about people issues, and then there are those lizards who only seem to care about performance issues. Look at Enron! Those guys counted their earnings practically every day and made loud, boastful statements to Wall Street about their performance. They compensated their highest performers with amazing, million-dollar bonuses regardless of how they achieved those results. It was insane! But did they ever bother to look deeply into the welfare of their people? No! Did they look at their behavioral incentive and reward systems, or question whether their people actually enjoyed coming to work or felt engaged or not? No! All they cared about was performance—getting more and more stuff done, and making more and more money. But look at the irony here; in the end, for Enron, it wasn't low performance that brought them down. What brought them down was low behavior. People issues! That invisible, ignored element in the execution mix that is more powerful than any other. It was the people issues, not performance, that brought them crashing down."

We sat in silence. Ravi was ranting and raving to the choir. We had agreed violently on this issue at least a hundred times.

An e-mail message popped onto my computer screen. It was my wife, Ruby, asking if I'd be meeting her for lunch. I looked at my watch and realized it was already past 1:00 P.M. Boy, time flies when your boss resigns! Ravi sensed the time issue and got up to leave. At the door, he turned around and waved at me, his signature rueful grin confident and back in full force.

"Let's stay in touch, okay?"

"Absolutely," I said, chuckling. "Maybe I'll see you at the next Bush Rat Toastmasters, huh?"

"Yeah, no kidding!" He rolled his eyes, and left.

I turned to my computer to shoot off a quick reply to Ruby. I told her I wouldn't be able to make it. I must admit, however, that I was not prepared for what I saw next. The e-mail message right after Ruby's was very short and succinct. It was from Deepak Amar, and it simply read:

Pelè Raymond Ugboajah, PhD

> *Mike,*
>
> *Thanks for your presentation today. As you know, we pride ourselves in offering for our own leaders, what we provide to our clients. We think you might benefit from some one-on-one executive coaching as a new director in our firm, so we would like to provide that offer to you. Please meet with Abigail Kapoor this afternoon at 3:00 P.M. to get started.*

Talk about an offer you couldn't refuse! I sat back for a few moments, took a deep breath, and then instinctively started tidying up my desk. I always did that when I was nervous. It was a way to calm my emotions. As they say, cleanliness is next to godliness. I needed a clean desk pretty badly at that point. I needed all the calmness I could muster to attend a one-on-one psychological coaching meeting with the biggest lizard I had ever known: Dr. Abigail Kapoor.

The Truth

I arrived at Abigail's corner office at exactly 3:00 P.M. and not a moment later. I didn't want a show of tardiness to worsen my predicament, especially since I wasn't sure exactly what I had done to warrant an executive coaching session with our most experienced industrial psychologist. I knew all too well the feeling of impending doom that would wash over the faces of those middle to senior executives that were "asked" by H.R. to come to LeaderTraits for a coaching session with Abigail. The request was usually couched in a statement that went something like this: "We have identified you as a high-potential employee, and we want you to begin some coaching sessions to increase your value to our company." It was never quite that simple. In truth, it was more often than not, a sign that upper management wanted to have a better insight into what was *wrong* with you, rather than what was great about you. The blank eyes and scared faces I saw were of people who were already mentally brushing up their resumes.

"Hello, Mike," Abigail said, in a surprisingly pleasant tone. "Sunny day out there, huh? How are you feeling this afternoon?"

"I'm doing great," I said, playing along with her attempt at warm and fuzzy chitchat. She motioned for me to sit on the couch next to her guest table. I obliged, and she sat down across her table from me. After seeing so many executives come and go, I had always wondered what it felt like to sit on Abigail's couch. Now I knew.

"That was an interesting presentation you gave today."

"Thanks."

"Let's be really informal about this," she began, holding up my H.R. file. "Tell me, how did you end up with a name like Mike Jordan?"

"I guess my parents gave it to me," I said, not hiding my sarcasm.

"That's interesting," she said. "I wonder, does your name put any pressure on you to be an overachiever like the real Mike Jordan?"

I considered her question. Was that the purpose of this meeting? Was I here so she could analyze my name? I thought I'd give her a deeper, more thoughtful response than before, just to play along with her.

"I think my name has in fact been an influence in my life. Growing up as an African-American guy with a name like that and not being able to play basketball to save my life, I suppose I may have developed some kind of complex about striving for excellence in something—anything. For me, that has so far been somewhere between music and motivational speaking."

"And what do you like the most about music and motivational speaking?"

"I like the fact that if you can practice the fundamentals, you can go very far. And I like the fact that you can go from not knowing a certain fundamental skill one day, and through disciplined, repetitive practice—like Michael Jordan or any other great performer—you can become really competent at it, and that competence can become second nature for you. I'm intrigued by the almost biological predictability inherent in practice. I guess the old saying is true: practice makes perfect."

"Nicely said," Abigail chirped. "Is that basically where you got your LeaderPractice concept?"

"I suppose there is an indirect connection," I admitted. "I believe that individual, team, or leadership behavior are learned competencies, just like sports, music, or public speaking. Certainly, we all start from different levels of talent and have different innate traits, but if we learn and practice enough, we can augment those traits and achieve any level of change or growth we desire."

"Right," she said, squinting her eyes and nodding as though she was impressed with my analysis. "Now, tell me, do you feel as though you are getting an opportunity to express yourself as a musician or a speaker here at LeaderTraits?"

I paused.

"Where is this going, Abigail?"

"Well, it seems that you are not happy here. It seems that you are not finding fulfillment and expression for the things that make you tick. Would that be an accurate assumption?"

I frowned and widened my eyes in a manner that suggested I was confused by her line of questioning. She picked up the H.R. file and continued.

"I have a copy of the initial psychological assessment you completed when you were hired, so we won't need a new inventory. I know that you have a proclivity toward excitability and that you are very creative; to the point where you believe that your ideas and innovations are worthy of adoption by others—whether they are aware of it or not. I also see here that you have a tendency to want to be liked and appreciated by others. In addition to being opinionated, you're ambitious and visionary, and with some work, you have the potential to be a solid leader."

At this point, my eyes had become riveted on the wood grains that ran through her oak desk. They were quite intricate, really. I began wondering how old the tree they were cut from must have been. Her voice had turned into a droning, steady cacophony.

"It also says here that you are..." Abigail paused. "Are you listening, Mike?'

"Yes," I said, looking up lazily at her. "Why am I really here, Abigail?" I asked, surprising even myself with my frankness. She put aside the H.R. file and leaned in toward me from across the table.

"Great question. I was hoping you could tell me that."

"What do you mean?"

"Why are you at LeaderTraits? Why aren't you out starting your own firm?"

I was taken aback by her question.

"Obviously, we can see that you are not happy here. You are consistently seeking and creating new, different ways that you think our business ought to be run. You are very innovative, in an environment where most of us are more...adaptive. I am just curious. Why *are* you here?"

I was still too surprised to respond.

"Have you heard of the Kirton continuum?" She asked.

"Yes."

"Then you should know that there are essentially two kinds of leaders—those who are adaptive and prefer to do things better and those who are innovative and prefer to do things differently. My guess is that you are the latter, and it frustrates you that we aren't adopting your new ideas. We're not changing as fast as you would want us to, are we?"

She had me at Kirton.

She leaned forward and placed a hand gently on my shoulder. There was a deceptively kind, nurturing look on her face. "I'm here to help you. Are you sure you really want to work here?"

The Three Gaps between Goals and Greatness

At that point, I snapped out of whatever pseudo-fugue state I was in and allowed myself a rare opportunity to speak freely. Not because I trusted her any more than I did previously, but because I had reached a threshold, and something had to give. I could smell a rat. This wasn't just another happy conversation between friends. It felt like a setup, and my reptilian emotions took over.

"Abigail, I think I know why I'm here on your couch. I'm here because you and others don't think I'm a good fit for this firm. I'm here because you think I have far too many new ideas, and I seem to be trying to sell them to you. Although you humor me and provided with me a title, the truth is that no one here really appreciates the fact that I want to bring change, especially in the way we do leadership development. No one seems to like the fact that I tend to speak my mind in meetings. It seems that my directness is not appreciated. I get all that. But my question to you is..."

I leaned closer until I was almost a foot from her face. The tear that began welling up in my eyes surprised me. "In your twenty-two years in business, is this how you treat people who challenge the status quo? Is this how you treat anyone who is not toeing the line precisely as written? Is firing people the only strategy you have for developing the kind of workforce you want? Is this how you teach our clients to encourage truth, positive ideas, and behavioral growth in their workforces? Is this how we helped Enron?"

I stood up abruptly and walked toward the door, opened it, and paused in the doorway. Turning back, I took a last, slow glance at the dark-haired, kind-looking, veteran industrial psychologist. I could see in her eyes, a certain steely resolve that must have served her well over all her years in business. She had a look on her face as though she had seen my type before—too much naiveté, ambition, and impatience.

"If this is how you do business," I said, "then let me save you the trouble of an exit interview." I closed her door gently and left the room.

I returned to my office and sent off an e-mail resignation to Abigail, Deepak, and the H.R. department. I hurriedly packed up my things and left my office. As I passed the front desk, I flashed Kelly the receptionist a goodnight smile. She smiled back and had a look on her face as though she couldn't understand why everyone was carrying cardboard boxes today. What she had no way of knowing is that, just like Ravi, the other guy with a cardboard box, this was my very last day at LeaderTraits.

Ruby

I could feel the sweat welling up in my palms as I headed west on Memorial Drive and then south onto the 610 loop. Blood rushed through my veins. My stomach had the kind of knot in it that was characteristic of whenever I was late for a class or an exam back in graduate school. In my mind, I played the text of Deepak's e-mail and Abigail's words over and over like the trailer of an upcoming horror movie. *I resigned!* Just like that. I was surprised by how well I followed my gut instinct. How long had their dissatisfaction with me been growing? Was this a direct result of Enron's collapse or Ravi's exit or was I on a previous short list? It didn't matter anymore. Nothing mattered. At this point, I could not imagine how on earth I was going to pay the bills. Like most American families, we were one paycheck away from poverty—just barely caught up with bills and living on credit. Although my wife, Ruby, normally could work whenever she wanted to as a locum tenens (traveling, substitute) physician, she was at that time on maternity leave after having our first child. With a brand new nursing baby, she certainly wasn't going to be traveling for long stretches of work any time soon.

I took the scenic, backstreet route to our middle-class, suburban home in Sugarland, partly to avoid the busy Houston traffic, and partly to consider my options. Every car that passed me seemed to feature a driver on a cell phone, and for some reason I could swear they all seemed to be angry and shouting at someone on the other end. What a rat race! Everyone seemed angry, or maybe I was seeing what I wanted to see, what I was feeling inside. *No wonder so many people hate their jobs.* With the possibility that you could lose your job at any time, for any reason—at will—how could anyone feel safe at work? How could anyone place the security and welfare of his or her family in the hands of untrustworthy, scheming, treacherous bosses? Baffled, I spent the drive home feeling a strange mixture of surprise, fear, and justified confusion. Not once did I follow my plan to consider the future, let alone what possible options might lie ahead.

I pulled into our garage at about 7:00 P.M. The door to the house was open. When I walked in, I saw Ruby sitting on the floor, reading a book, with a balloon tied to her long, wavy hair. *Yes*—on the floor with a balloon tied to her hair!

Ruby was a dark-skinned, Trinidadian beauty I had been lucky to meet on a business trip to the Midwest some seven years prior. Once you got to know her, you quickly learned that sitting on the floor was no big deal. She was a creature of the earth: natural, spiritual, and uninhibited. No need for chairs when the floor was right there! At the hospital where she worked, she was known as the *funny* doctor—the physician who always brought smiles to a patient's face. Whether she was wearing a balloon or a flower on her head, she knew how to lift spirits, even if it meant sitting on the floor with a scared pediatric patient. The book in her hand was turned to a page near the end. Ruby was an incredibly fast reader and sharp as nails. I therefore assumed she must have just started that book an hour or so earlier.

"Hey, your energy's low. What's up?" She asked, with a big, oversized smile on her face.

"Nothing." I wasn't prepared to spoil her mood quite yet. "How're you and the baby?"

"Just ducky!" she quipped. After almost seven years of marriage, I had never really gotten used to her individualized, geeky language. She had been kind enough to explain to me the method behind her occasional, mad responses to questions like that. If you asked her how she was doing, instead of the standard answer, she'd proudly tell you her height: five-feet-four-inches-thank-you! If you asked how things were or inquired after her welfare, she'd say either "Okay," which meant, not that great. If she'd say "Just ducky," it meant she was as good as it gets. If she agreed with you on something, she might say, "Cool beans," and if you ever made the mistake of asking her "You know what?" she'd say, "Chicken butt!" She was a special soul—sometimes moody, usually fun loving, and always sincere and transparent in her emotions.

Obviously, all had gone well for her so far that day.

"I just quit my job," I said.

"Great," she said, showing no shock in response to my statement. "So now you can spend some quality time with me and Junior."

"Ruby, I'm not kidding. We're broke, and finding a new job in this economy is not going to be easy."

"Great, so now you can write that leadership book you've been dawdling about." Ruby liked to use colorful words routinely. I can't tell you how many cool words like *dawdling* she had introduced into my lexicon. I remember when we first met, and she had used the word *circuitous* to describe her journey through medical school. I was so impressed with her I married her.

"Honey, I'm serious. If I hadn't quit today, I'm pretty sure they would have fired me anyway. I think this Enron disaster is turning the whole company upside down. Even the CEO, Ravi, quit just hours before I did! And he was my greatest supporter. Frankly, I had two professional choices left at LeaderTraits—be uncomfortable or unemployed!"

"Great, so now you can follow your heart," she said. "Let's see, there's music, public speaking, entrepreneurship…"

I gave up. Despite my explanations, she certainly wasn't going to let me have my pity party! I hung up my sport coat and dragged myself upstairs to see how Junior was doing. Upstairs in our middle-class, suburban home, looking down at our two-week-old son in his crib, I couldn't help but wonder what kind of world we had brought him into. Certainly, I would try to do everything in my power to provide for him, but what happens when things are out of my control? What happens when you do everything you thought you needed to do to be successful, and you still fall short? I sat down and watched him breathe. I could hear his little nostrils consuming the air around him. I was so exhausted that I didn't realize when I was mercifully overcome by sleep.

The Brain Conspiracy

"Whoa!" I shouted, jumping up in surprise from the touch on my shoulder. It was Ruby.

"Pretty sharp fight-or-flight response there!" she said, smiling. "Aren't you hungry?"

I followed her back downstairs and threw myself on a chair at the dinner table. I could still feel the sweat on my palms. The abrupt way my job ended was still fresh on my mind.

"What will we do for money?" I groaned. "It takes an average of nine months in this economy to find a new job."

Ruby flopped some lasagna onto my plate and responded to my question with a totally unrelated question of her own. Always the doctor, she was probably trying to help me break the negative cycle of my thoughts.

"What was that new brain-based theory you said you were developing?"

"LeaderPractice," I said, playing along.

"Tell me about it."

"Why?"

"Because that's what you're going to do for the next nine months, right?"

She was right. One could argue that, with a bit of positive thinking, this job loss could be repositioned as my best chance to flesh out my theories into a viable consulting offering. Maybe I could even run it by Ravi and gauge his interest in helping me sell it to new customers.

"Are you sure you can handle my rambling?" Proselytizing was second nature for me.

"Try me," she said, dishing out her food and taking a seat next to me.

"Okay. At the core of the LeaderPractice concept is the idea that you have to think of people as brains—big brains with arms and legs." I motioned with my two hands, as though I were holding a massive ball in the air. "As such, any theory of workplace learning or development has to first take into account the default ways in which people's brains work." I felt a good, warm rush of positive emotion inside. I was always in my element when I was in teacher mode.

"So, are you saying that LeaderPractice is about hypnotizing people into learning or behaving a certain way?" Ruby crossed her eyes as she spoke, her mouth stuffed full of lasagna.

"No, silly! I'm saying that LeaderPractice is really about learning through repetition and practice because that's the way our brains work. It's about learning behavioral skills so well that they become habits in our brains, just like learning to play the piano or to ride a bike or to become a better public speaker. Turning skills into habits is the magic formula for creating lasting behavioral change in organizations."

"So what's the big deal?" Ruby asked. "Why does anyone need lasting behavioral change?" She enjoyed her role as my critic and devil's advocate. She knew she did it well and that it helped me iron out my thoughts. This little exercise was more for me than it was for her.

"Well," I said, happy to launch into a full-fledged lecture. "Let me show you what I mean with a picture." I pulled out my iPhone, opened a sketch app, and drew the following diagram for her:

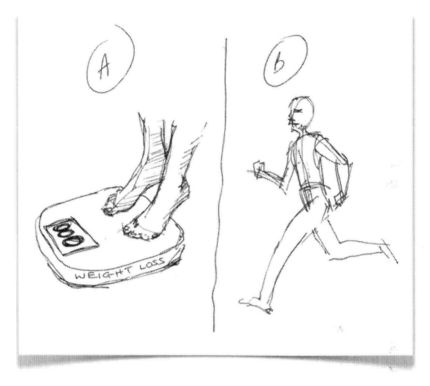

"Imagine you wanted lasting weight loss, and you had two choices—either you exclusively measure yourself everyday and do nothing else, or you exclusively exercise. Which strategy is more likely to result in weight loss?"

"None!" she said. "No, I'm just kidding. Obviously, you have to exercise. Measuring won't do much for you, except potentially increase your frustration."

"Exactly!" I said. "And yet, this is actually what most organizations do. They focus on the weight scale, which only measures the outcomes they want such as performance, sales, etc.

But they don't invest as much time into measuring and addressing the things that *cause* those outcomes in the first place. For weight loss, you'd focus on measuring and improving your eating and exercise habits. In an organization, in addition to looking at the visible scales of sales and employee performance, you'd want to concurrently measure the major contributor to high performance— the behavior element—of both employees and leaders."

"How interesting!" Ruby said, which felt like a great accomplishment. She wasn't the easiest person to sell ideas to.

"At the end of the day," I said, "firing every employee who struggles behaviorally is a dumb workforce development strategy. Lasting behavioral change among employees, teams, and leaders is what our clients really want. That's how they build a predictable culture of success. The psychological assessments we give them are really just tools to be used toward that end. Also, behavior is elastic. Most of us have established behavioral patterns that we tend to return to, no matter how much we try to change. It's almost as if the brain is constantly conspiring to return us to our comfort zones, our realms of safety. If, for example, you were a micromanager at work, and your actions were destroying your team's efforts to create success, you're not going to be able to change that behavior easily just because we give you an assessment that tells you this or that is your problem. And you're certainly not going to change that behavior by going to a seminar. The only way you can change that behavior is through repetitive practice until you physically change the biology of your brain. And the only way you can achieve that kind of lasting behavioral change would be to use the LeaderPractice process."

"Which is?"

"Still just a concept," I admitted, rolling my eyes, and realizing that she'd just helped me expose the unfinished state of my theory.

"There you go!" Ruby said, happy that she'd gotten my mind on a different trajectory. "Sounds like you've got work to do!"

"Yeah, after I get a new job," I said, snapping back to reality.

"Oh no, you won't!"

"What?"

"I don't want you to get another job."

For the first time since I got home, I could sense that Ruby was serious. She stood up from the table, staring at me with arms akimbo. She wasn't playing the funny doctor anymore.

"Is your brain conspiring to return you to your comfort zone?"

Her question gave me pause. She was right. I was demonstrating the same brain conspiracy I had just lectured her about.

"Honey," she said, less challenging this time, "I really want you to take some time off and reflect on this whole thing. Please don't rush back into another job. You know you'd rather not, anyway. Junior and I really need you to be centered and happy again. I can always request some additional hours at a hospital. We can get by, honey."

"But what about right now? The mortgage? The bills?"

"We can use our savings. Let the bills go unpaid for a couple of months. It'll be cool beans. We'll be just ducky!"

Maybe she was right. Maybe what I really needed was to abandon my comfort zone and get away from employee mode for a while. Maybe I needed time to just innovate. Just do some good old entrepreneurial dreaming again. For all of my professional years I had battled with the age-old struggle of what to become when I grew up: employee or entrepreneur. Right then, at that moment, I felt the entrepreneur slowly crawling out of hiding. The light bulbs started to go off in my head. I began to think of a million things that I'd have to do to firm up my new theory and prepare it for prospective firms. Hello world! My entrepreneurial passion had reawakened!

Pelè Raymond Ugboajah, PhD

    "You know what?" I asked in a calm voice.

    "Chicken butt!" she joked.

    "I love you, Dr. Ruby Jordan."

    "I know," she said, and started putting away the dishes.

Uff Dah!

few days after I left LeaderTraits, I looked up my old Toastmasters club online and decided to stop by one evening. It is always awkward to rejoin your old club. I had joined Toastmasters a few years back but hadn't visited in a long time. Whenever you finally make it back, a part of you is excited to see old friends, who hopefully, are still there. However, another part of you is concerned about those who might think that you're somewhat of a traitor because you *got too busy* for the group in the first place. I decided that, regardless of the potential criticisms, I needed a place to talk through my emotions. I also needed to get back into public speaking, a passion that had never truly left me, even as an employee. For me, Toastmasters was like safe, anonymous group therapy. I could work things out in my mind, share them with total strangers, give and receive applauses and prizes, and feel a whole lot better on the way home.

Our club was known as the Tiny Apple Toastmasters of Houston. We held our meetings weekly at the downtown real estate office of Coldwell Banker Burnett. Each week, you could expect to see anywhere from ten to fifteen members in attendance. Sometimes you'd see the occasional guest visiting for the first time. On the evening I showed up, I saw a few familiar faces and a lot more new ones. I felt like a brand new guest all over again.

"Madam Toastmaster!" shouted Charlie, our club president. He was a gray old man with impeccable taste in suits.

We all rose, clapping, as Margie, our toastmaster for the day, walked up and took her position at the lectern. She called the meeting to order.

"Mr. President, fellow toastmasters, new guests, and especially Mike Jordan, our long-lost, returning toastmaster!"

Everyone clapped. A Toastmasters club is the only place I know of on this planet where folks will clap for you for absolutely no reason whatsoever. I soaked it in, beaming at everyone.

"Today," Margie continued. "We're going to do things a little differently. Instead of the usual extemporaneous table-topics format, we're going to ask volunteers to just come up and give a two-minute speech on the topic of their choice. However, there is one caveat—the speech has to be funny, meaningful, and completely unplanned!" The group swelled in a hushed murmur.

"Who would like to go first?"

Silence. I looked at the faces of the people in attendance. Charlie sat way in the back, clad in one of his impeccable suits. Larry, whom we affectionately called Mr. Nervous, sat in front of me. To my right was Anna, the oldest and most loyal Toastmaster I had ever met, and to my left was Akosua, the Ghanaian woman who had recently immigrated to the United States with her family. Everyone remained silent.

"I'll go!" I said, hoping to wake our group from its slumber.

"No, Mike," said Margie, a firm look on her face, as if to say I should know better.

"Let's let current members go first."

I was shocked! I always knew Margie liked to be in solid control whenever it was her turn to be toastmaster, but I never thought she had it in her to publicly embarrass anyone. I tucked my bruised ego back into my pocket and slowly lowered my hand.

The Three Gaps between Goals and Greatness

"Who wants to get us started?" She asked.

"I will," said Mr. Nervous. It was a pleasant surprise to see him bravely accept the challenge. I didn't realize he had overcome his extreme fear of public speaking so quickly. The last time I saw him speak he was a wreck, but to our mixed responses of respect and amazement, he had promised us that he would someday become a great speaker. He also asked everyone to always call him Mr. Nervous, so that he could stay inspired and continue working hard to get over his fear of public speaking. I took out my notebook and a pen to write my evaluation notes and observations.

Mr. Nervous arrived at the lectern and hugged it for dear life, quietly trying to calm his nerves over what seemed like an eternity. Gazing at something above and behind the audience, he took a deep breath and finally began to speak.

"I am not a very funny man," he said. "But I'm workin' on it."

Everyone laughed and clapped for him. As I said, if you want to get some supportive applause, come to a meeting of the Tiny Apple Toastmasters.

"One day, when I was walking my dog, a cat came over and hissed at us. My dog turned around and barked at it. I looked at them as they quarreled in their different languages, not understanding each other, and I realized, this must be how we humans are. We fight and we quarrel every day all over the world with people we barely understand, and somehow we think we're right. Well, we're not. I know, because neither that cat nor my dog was right. I joined them and without saying a word, I knelt down, and started stroking them gently and lovingly, begging them both to stop. Amazingly, they did, and I didn't have to speak English, dog, or cat to get my point across. And that's why since that day, I've always wondered if the lingua franca in animal world…is love."

The room erupted in claps and cheers! Mr. Nervous had become a master toastmaster, just like he told us he would! The last time I heard him speak, sweat was running down his face, he stumbled through every line, *uummed* and *aaahhed* his way through every phrase, and made absolutely no logical or emotional point whatsoever at the end of his speech. I remember feeling sorry for him and thinking he had to be the most nervous speaker I had ever heard. What an impressive improvement - after only a few months of focused practice! I was so impressed, I started taking notes on what I had just observed.

"Wow!" Margie said, walking over to the lectern. "Who wants to try following that?" She shot me a stern look as if to say, don't you dare! I kept still, and obeyed her eyes.

"I will!" someone said. It was Akosua, the immigrant from Ghana. From her first few words, I could tell that her English had dramatically improved. She stood up and strode behind the lectern.

"Fellow toastmasters, it has been a long, difficult journey for my husband Kofi and I. Over the past two years, we have had to learn English, learn a new culture, and help people understand that we are not related to U.N. secretary general Kofi Annan."

She got a nice round of laughter and applause for that one.

"But ever since we joined this group, some of our friends from back home keep asking why we have sold out to America. They want to know why we are working so hard to learn this new American language and assimilate into the culture, especially when things are improving back home. We have talked until we are blue in the face, and every time we meet these people, we have only one answer for them—we did not abandon our culture in exchange for this one. We are proud to still cherish our roots. But we keep telling them that this is the land of the free. We are free. We may originally hail from Africa, but today, we are proud to say that we are also Americans."

The Three Gaps between Goals and Greatness

Everyone stood up. She got more than applause—she got a prolonged, standing ovation. I watched her walk back to her seat, and I could just make out the newly formed tears in her eyes.

Charlie spoke next and gave us a stirring story about his childhood dreams, and how he had made most of them come true, especially the one about getting over his stammering.

"You might not realize that I was once a massive stammerer, especially since I'm such a great speaker now." We clapped for him, and he stood there, beaming and waiting for the audience applause to subside. Once we stopped clapping, he continued.

"But what each and everyone of you knows is that, in my fifteen years as a toastmaster, a week has not gone by without me standing in front of a mirror and practicing my lines. I stand here today, speaking fluidly and confidently, not because I'm better than the next guy, but because I believed in myself. I knew I could do it. I just knew that if I kept trying, over and over again, that someday, I'd learn how to say s-s-s-stammering, without actually doing so, Madam Toastmaster!"

He got his second applause and took a seat. And so, they went round the room, giving every member an opportunity to speak. Anna talked about her best friend, Rosalyn, who passed away a few months back, expressing confidence that they would meet again soon. Margie closed the meeting with a stirring speech about her son's recent diagnosis of schizophrenia. I am not sure there was a dry eye in the room after her speech.

"And with that," Margie said, with a smile, "I would like to bring our meeting to a close. But first, can we invite our long-lost guest to comment on our meeting today?"

I was a little surprised by her late invitation. In fact, I almost concluded she hadn't wanted me to speak at all. At the end of a meeting, it is normal to ask new guests if they'd be interested in sharing their observations about the meeting they had just witnessed. I just didn't think I'd be regarded literally as a new member. In any case, I was so engrossed in the beautiful stories from these wonderful people that I totally forgot about my initial need to talk out my emotions. I walked up to the lectern and moved it out of the way. I looked each person in the eye at least once before I started to speak, fueling a pregnant pause before my abrupt beginning.

"Fellow toastmasters!" I announced. "My name is Mike Jordan. Please raise your hands—how many of you have heard of Mike Jordan, the greatest basketball player on earth?"

Everyone raised a hand.

"Well I'm not he!" I proclaimed. The group laughed and clapped for me. Even Margie was beaming. It was a cheap shot, but I got my laugh anyway.

"Uff dah," I continued, "is an exclamation used in the upper Midwest where my wife Ruby works as a physician. It is a Scandinavian and Norwegian-born slang that is used to show surprise, extreme joy, or as an exclamation when someone feels overwhelmed by something. Uff dah is how I felt when I walked in here and saw old friends, fellow toastmaster competitors, and most importantly, when I saw the progress that so many of you have made as speakers. As I watched you work together, struggle together, and grow successful speaking habits together, I realized that practicing on your own doesn't come close to the power of practicing within a supportive community environment like Toastmasters."

"I also realized that in addition to community there are three important requirements for true learning to occur. Those three requirements are a focus on results, reasons, and repetition." I saw the first requirement in Mr. Nervous. By golly, he set a clear goal for himself, and he announced it to all of us, almost as a challenge to himself. Then he achieved every part of that goal. I saw the next requirement in Akosua, who has remained motivated and found enormous success in the United States because for her, becoming an American was personally and emotionally powerful. The third requirement is evident in Charlie, who knew that through repetition, he could learn or overcome anything he set his heart to."

"I wrote these three Rs down as you spoke: results, reasons, and repetition, and I realized that you have given me a most powerful gift today. Believe it or not, what I have learned from you here will someday help fuel my entrepreneurial dreams. What your community environment does for speaking practice can work miracles for my passion, leadership practice! So, if you don't mind, I would like to show you my awe, happiness, and absolute appreciation by saying uff dah!"

Everyone clapped. I took my applause, said good-bye to everyone, and quietly headed for home.

Pelè Raymond Ugboajah, PhD

Breakfast with Ruby

The next morning, I awoke to find Ruby fully dressed in black and red, her favorite color combination. She had once told me that only in combination do these colors mean she is happy. If she ever wore black alone, it meant she was feeling sad. If she ever wore red, it meant she was feeling powerful. But if she ever wore them together—watch out, world because it meant that she was feeling really good inside.

"Let's go out for breakfast!" she announced.

"What about Junior?" I asked.

"He's just ducky! The neighbors' daughter Sarah agreed to babysit for us. She's downstairs."

"So what brought this on? I see you're wearing your positive feelings today."

"I think we should go do a summit," she replied.

I nodded, thoughtfully considering her proposal. Ever since we'd been married, we had made it an annual practice to go somewhere far away from our usual daily lives and talk about our future, our dreams, our goals, and how things were going in our minds and hearts. We called this our yearly summit, and it's almost like a business meeting where we, as heads of our household, would enter into treaties and agreements for the future.

"Let's do it!" I said.

"Cool beans!" she said

I took a quick shower and threw on my dark blue suit. After kissing Junior good-bye and thanking Sarah, we drove south on Highway forty-five, all the way to Galveston, where we stopped at La Ruca, our favorite restaurant. It was a small place on Seawall Boulevard, and it featured an excellent view of the ocean, with the waves splashing in from the Gulf of Mexico. We sat outside on the patio, and the cool, morning breeze quickly engulfed us. Our waiter brought us some coffee, and we began our summit.

"Okay," I said. "You go first. Let's start with right now. What's good, and what's bad?"

Ruby looked away, avoiding my gaze. "No, you start," she said.

"All right then," I said, taking a large swig of my coffee. "Right now, what's good is that even though I'm unemployed, I'm actually pretty excited about my new theory on leadership practice."

"You mean, *hypothesis*, Ruby interjected. "It's not proven yet."

"Yeah, whatever!" I exclaimed playfully. Ruby was always exacting about semantics. "Anyway," I continued, "I've been doing a lot of research on brain-based learning and communities of practice, and my Toastmasters visit yesterday only further confirmed for me that this is a powerful and viable idea. I think I'm going to call Ravi and see if he'll partner with me someday on a new management consulting firm."

"Great," Ruby said. "So what's bad?"

"Obviously, what's bad is that I have to find a job in the meantime."

"No, honey, we talked about that!" Ruby jumped in, a concerned frown on her face. "You were going to take some time off and hang out more with me and Junior, right? Remember? You were going to work on your entrepreneurial dream, right?"

I chuckled. "You're right. In that case, everything's great. Your turn!"

"Well, I got some tough news yesterday," she said. "But I didn't want to bother you with it." She was still avoiding my eyes.

"Go ahead," I said. "This is what our summits are for."

"LocumDoctors called to tell me that they can't schedule me for work near Houston anymore."

"Why is that?"

"Their contracts weren't renewed by the area hospitals because they are all being bought up by some big, national health care conglomerate. Without a contract, they can't schedule me at any hospital around here."

"So what does that mean? How will you get work?"

"They can still schedule me in Middleville, which is the only other city where they still have a viable contract."

"Are you okay with going up there more often?" I asked. Ruby had never really enjoyed flying.

"That's what I want to talk to you about."

"Go for it," I said.

"I think we need to move up there."

"You mean sell our house?"

"Yep!"

"And go live up there in that cold, winter wonderland?"

"Yep!"

"No-o-oh way!" I sputtered. "I'd rather work at a Burger King here in Houston."

Ruby turned away again, slowly, her hair covering her face. I leaned in to get a closer look at her. Surely my joke wasn't *that* funny. Indeed, it turned out not to have been very funny at all. When I pushed her hair gently from her eyes, I found that she was in tears.

"Honey, what's wrong?" I whispered. She wouldn't answer me. Instead, her tears flowed more freely, and she began to sob and shake.

"What is it, honey? Look, if this is about my need to go get a job—"

"No!" she growled, looking around the restaurant with a guilty look on her face, as if she was hoping no one else had seen her show of emotion. "It's not always about you. This is about me!"

"Okay then," I said, instinctively knowing it was time to back off. "What's going on?"

"I'm a failure!" she said, in between her sobs.

"What?"

"I feel as though I've failed myself. I've failed you, and now, Junior, as well."

"Honey, you're not making any sense," I said.

"Ever since I quit residency, this problem has kept coming back to haunt me. If I had just finished that darn residency program, maybe we'd have our choice of hospitals or locum tenens firms right now. Maybe I'd be a licensed neurosurgeon somewhere. At this rate, I won't even be able to feed my family! This is why I'm a failure!"

I held her close and wiped her tears. No words were necessary. Ruby had always held this chip on her shoulder. No matter what I told her about how great a doctor she was or how appreciated she was at every hospital she ever worked, she just couldn't shake her own feelings of personal and professional inadequacy. Always doubting herself, always striving to improve her already stellar performance as a doctor, Ruby just couldn't find a way to believe fully in herself, no matter what the overwhelming evidence showed.

"Honey, we've talked about this. Every hospital you've ever worked at has validated that you are a success. Not only are you technically good at your craft as a physician, you're also excellent on the people side. Your patients love you, and your colleagues love working with you. How on earth could you be a failure? I'm lucky to be married to one of the best doctors I've ever known!"

The Three Gaps between Goals and Greatness

"Thanks," she said, wiping her tears. "Maybe I'm being unreasonable. It's just that every time we get into these binds, I feel like it's my fault for not having more options for us."

Silence. I thought about her words for what seemed like an eternity. We just sat there in silence. What she was suggesting would mean nothing short of a complete relocation of our family from Houston to some remote, cold, small town of less than five thousand people in the midwestern heartland. Besides the obvious culture shock, what would I do for a job? Even if I did start an entrepreneurial venture, where would I find customers, especially since the hospital was the only actual "business" in town? I tried hard to picture myself as Mr. Dad, Mr. Stay-at-home father, but it didn't work. I just didn't know how it *could* work. But I trusted Ruby. I knew that if she felt this strongly about something, then it wasn't trivial. I also knew that the reality we currently faced was palpable. I had no income, and now, neither did she, unless we moved to the small town of Middleville, where work was possible for her. I nodded my head, as if coming to a place of mental clarity.

"If you really think we should move, then maybe we should," I said.

"Honey, it's not that I think we should move," she said. "We have no choice."

Pelè Raymond Ugboajah, PhD

Voodoo

The voice on the other line was muffled, as though it was answering me from halfway across the world. "This is Ravi."

"Hi, Ravi," I said. "Are you in town?"

"No way! I'm in Cancun! Life is good! I'm on a beach, sipping a piña colada!"

"Wow!" I said. "Listen, can we talk?"

"Sure, what's going on?"

"I quit LeaderTraits."

"I heard," he said. "I told you that you were a bush rat trying to survive in a lizard's world!"

I ignored his unfunny joke. "Ravi, I need your help."

"How can I help you, Mike?"

"Would you be willing to partner with me to start a new company?"

He exploded in laughter. Mixed with ocean waves and phone static, laughter can sound quite eerie.

"Listen," he said. I didn't mean to crack up that way, but I've always admired your audacity! We can't continue this conversation right now. Call me in about an hour at my hotel. I'm staying at the

Ritz-Carlton, and I'll have better reception there. I can't promise you I'll be interested, but I'll certainly hear you out."

Click.

Ignoring his outburst and abrupt exit, I nonetheless resigned myself to any opportunity to speak with him. Ravi was a huge success, financially and personally. His perspective on my new ideas would be invaluable, even if he didn't want to be involved. Not only would it be a great blessing and a gift if Ravi were interested in starting a new firm with me, it would possibly make my career. He was a solid leader who could sell anything, and I felt that his presence (I hoped as CEO) would practically guarantee the success of whatever we would collaborate on.

I put the phone down on the empty floor and went downstairs to see how the movers were doing. The house was practically empty at this point, except for a few major pieces of furniture such as my piano and recording studio equipment in the basement. I had asked them to move those last so that we could be extra careful with them. When I got downstairs, I found Ruby holding Junior in her left arm and issuing orders to the movers with her right hand. She was explaining and clarifying her instructions, making sure they knew exactly where and how to position her kitchen teapots, china, and other delicate pieces in their truck. Six men from the moving company had been working nonstop for about two hours now, packing and moving boxes into a huge truck. Their trip from Houston to the upper Midwest would be a 1,500-mile journey that they planned to break up into two days. Ruby and I planned to get everything packed, ship our car, and then catch a flight up there. So far, we had put our home on the market and hired a realtor to help us sell it. Things were moving fast. We were ready to leave Houston and begin a new phase of our lives,

An hour later, I called Ravi again. This time, our phone reception was excellent; he sounded as clear as though he might be in the next empty room of my house.

"Thanks for taking the time to speak with me, Ravi."

"Not a problem, bush rat. Glad to help."

We laughed briefly together.

"I'm curious," I said. "What did you hear about why I left LeaderTraits?"

"I heard that you quit before you got fired. Good move! It could have happened anytime because frankly, those guys can't handle change. They thrive on things remaining the way they've always been. But I wouldn't worry about LeaderTraits. After you and I left, two other senior consultants left as well, and that started an avalanche of further resignations. After that, I heard that several big clients wanted nothing to do with them because of their tight Enron affiliation, so customers started leaving. Right now, I think they're back to a two-person psychological assessment shop, just Deepak and Abigail like the old days!"

"Wow," I said. "No more leaders or clients at LeaderTraits? They might as well just change their name to Traits!"

Ravi chuckled. "I think the danger signs were clearly there, but they couldn't see them," he said. "The fact is you can't just build a business telling people what they want to hear in the form of psychological assessments. You've got to help organizations make the shift from the performance paradigm to the behavior paradigm. If we had done more over the years to help Enron's people develop a different kind of culture, who knows if this would have happened?"

"Exactly," I said, seizing my opportunity to talk about my new venture. "This is exactly why I think we should start a new firm that focuses more on helping organizations create lasting behavioral change—"

Ravi interrupted me. "Okay, I meant to repeat my apology for bursting out in laughter when you mentioned that before. I really do appreciate your audacity and I think it will take you far. But I have to be honest—it would be extremely presumptuous of you to think I'd be interested in doing a start-up with you. Just because I hired you into a director position at LeaderTraits doesn't mean you've magically become partner material or that you've now got what it takes to run your own leadership development firm. You've never even been at the leadership table as a vice president of a firm! Frankly, I'm just not into theory and postulation—I'm into sales. If it don't sell, then it ain't swell—got it?"

"But—"

"No, seriously! I will gladly listen to your ideas, and maybe even give you my perspective from a real-world point of view, but don't insult me by thinking I'd even be remotely interested in starting a new business with you! That's truly audacious!"

Silence. His voice had become so loud that I almost thought he was actually in the room with me. I had known Ravi to sometimes play the role of the abrasive, arrogant leader, but he had never addressed me in such a scathing and bitter manner. I gathered my thoughts and tried to break the impasse.

"Ravi, will you at least hear me out?"

"Sure, shoot."

"Okay. First, you should know that Ruby and I are moving to the Midwest, to Middleville, where her hospital is."

"Congratulations."

"Well, it's less of an accomplishment than a necessity. We need to be closer so she can get consistent work now that we're a one-income family. But this means I probably will have no choice but to start an entrepreneurial venture since it's a town of only five thousand people, and the only business in town is the hospital."

"That's great! At least you'll have some time off and freedom to work on your new ideas."

"Exactly, and I would love it if you'd at least listen to my concepts before you write them off."

Ravi paused and said, "Sure, I'm glad to listen. Go ahead. But here's a programming note—I have a Cancun tour coming up in a few minutes, so I will have to end this call really soon. Pretend we're on an elevator, and you've got to sell me on this thing. What is the premise? Why should I care?"

"Great," I said. I had no problem with a challenge like that. If anything, now I had his full attention. "Okay, you and I agree fully that one of the problems in the way we deliver our management consulting services to the corporate world is the lack of follow-up. In other words, we sell companies like Enron a bunch of psychological assessments, but we don't do much to help their people develop lasting changes that will actually make a difference, right?"

"Right."

"Okay, and we agree that the real problem in organizations is that they have a bunch of plans, but their execution of those plans is really where the problem lies, right?"

"Right."

"Good," I said. "That's where my new theory comes in. It is a well-known concept that the real problem organizations want to solve is the issue of closing that execution gap—how to turn all their plans and goals into success and ultimately, greatness. But there is an even more insidious, hidden problem."

"And what's that, professor?"

I chuckled. "The real problem is that far too many companies don't realize that execution involves not only performance outcomes but also the combined behavior of all their individuals, teams, and leaders that creates whatever culture they end up with.

Because they spend all of their time focusing on increasing performance outputs, critical behavior inputs go unchecked, and can lead to the kind of culture and disaster we just saw at Enron."

"Okay, genius," Ravi said. "How do you solve that problem?"

"Well, that's not all. Not only do companies pay lip service to the behavior paradigm, their leaders don't do much about it, so that even though they agree with all the three-step, five-step, and twelve-step programs that management consultants are selling them, they never actually implement anything or create more productive habits. Instead, executives often try winging leadership, which usually means reverting to destructive behavioral comfort zones. And finally, even when people do try to change their behavior for the benefit of the organization, they end up doing so in isolation, and they suck up to their bosses so that they can get good evaluations and bonuses. Organizations rarely create opportunities to socialize the behavior-improvement process. It stays individual, and when people don't have any personal or communal incentive, their change efforts usually just peter out over time."

"Mike, you've got like twenty seconds left. All you've told me so far is the problem. What's the solution?"

"Here's the solution, Ravi. I think that there are three gaps between an organization's goals and its greatness—not just the one, monolithic execution gap everyone talks about. I think that there is the behavior gap, the habits gap, and the community gap. If you can close the behavior gap by measuring and improving behavior at the same level of granularity that people do for performance, you'll be closer to success. And if you can help people create success habits — not just acknowledge the things they know they should change— then you're closer to success. And finally, if you can leverage a community of practice—like Toastmasters—where people come together to grow together, then you're really onto something!"

The Three Gaps between Goals and Greatness

"Okay, time's up!" Ravi screamed. "I've got to go. But here's some feedback for you. I'm sorry I'm not being a very nice guy right now, but the fact is, I don't see any money in this thing. When you first talked about it at LeaderTraits, I liked the simple parable about how practice makes perfect, which I thought you were introducing. But now I'm not so sure I know where you're going with all of this. Don't get me wrong—it sounds like an interesting theory, and it might even someday become a great idea, but I can't sell theories to clients. Right now, it's all voodoo. I can't sell *voodoo*. You haven't yet shown me the money. So as far as I'm concerned, unless you can somehow prove to me that this theory will work in real life, there is not much to talk about. Remember, if it don't sell, then it ain't swell! Enjoy your trip to the cold Midwest, Mike!"

Click.

"What a nice guy," I said out loud, boiling with sarcasm and still holding the phone to my ear. I put down the receiver and returned mentally to the empty room in which I sat. I looked out the window at the neighbors' houses and beyond, at the hundreds and thousands of similar-looking box homes and red roofs in our suburban Sugarland neighborhood. I could hear the sounds of the movers hauling out the last items from our house, and I could also make out Ruby's voice, calming down Junior while simultaneously issuing commands.

No matter what I thought about his arrogant delivery, Ravi had a point. I had a theory but no proof. How on earth could I get a seasoned sales leader like Ravi interested in my concepts? What would I need to do to show him that this was a viable idea? Never one to back down from a challenge, I started to see this as an opportunity. Surely, if someone as arrogant and pragmatic as Ravi could ever see the viability of my ideas, then we would have a fighting chance in the open market. I began formulating a commitment to put everything I had into this thing. I would throw my mind, my heart, and indeed my very soul into proving the validity of my ideas. I would show him that this wasn't voodoo.

I walked downstairs and gave Ruby and Junior a big hug. The movers were loaded and ready to head out. We stepped outside and stood in front of our empty house, watching them drive away with our lives. In the next few days we'd be living in Middleville: small-town USA! I looked at Ruby and Junior, and wondered what was in store for us. Ruby rested her head on my shoulder. We had no way of knowing just how much our lives were about to change. I gave Ruby another big hug and quietly whispered in her ear, "Uff dah!"

Part 2: The Goals

Pelè Raymond Ugboajah, PhD

Middleville

"You betcha!" said Emily Watson, in her thick midwestern accent. She was head realtor at Moose Lake Realtors, Inc., and she had just responded to my inquiry about whether someone could show us some homes for rent or sale in Middleville. "Yah, sure," she announced over the phone. "I'll be right over to pick you up!"

Ruby and I had arrived in Middleville a few days before, full of hope and anticipation for an opportunity to settle down and get our family back on track. Ruby insisted that I take some time off from employment altogether, just to dream and regroup. In her case, she was glad for a chance to work more hours in a stable shift at one hospital, as opposed to traveling across country working at multiple locations. Since we arrived, we had kept our things in storage and stayed at the Middleville Motel, a small mom-and-pop outfit located just a few blocks south of Main Street in the city's central business district.

Middleville was a beautiful little tourist town nestled between two valleys in Larson County. People would come from all over the Midwest to fish, hunt, and enjoy its many lakes and scenic, wooded spaces. The city itself was home to about five thousand people, although many in the community feared that more people were leaving the city than moving into it. As the young graduated from the only high school in town and left for jobs in bigger cities, many feared that they simply wouldn't come back to Middleville. They feared that someday, the town could end up being populated exclusively by old people. Of course, the fact that there was really only one business in town did not help. The Middleville Hospital was by far the largest employer in town, with about 100 full-time employees. The sword of Damocles hanging over Middleville residents was the thought of the hospital closing. If that were ever to happen, it would certainly mean that Middleville would become a ghost town, not unlike the fate of nearby Lakewater, which was once a booming gold town in the late 1900s—until there was no more gold. Despite these fears, Middleville was a place of hope, close-knit families, and a certain, celebrated thick skin for surviving anything, including the Midwest's well-known, treacherous winters.

My phone rang, and Emily asked us to meet her outside the motel. Ruby, Junior, and I put on our jackets and headed out. Even though it was late September, we had heard enough about the unpredictable midwestern weather to make sure we stayed better safe than sorry.

"Dr. Ruby!" proclaimed Emily. Admiration was written all over her face. She hugged my wife profusely and made goo-goo faces at Junior. "And you must be Dr. Ruby's husband!" She said, looking at me.

I nodded with a smile, quietly accepting my new moniker. She turned back to Ruby and said, "You probably don't remember me, Dr. Ruby, but you were the doctor who helped bring my aunt back to life when she suffered a heart attack."

Ruby smiled, as though she had experienced this scene a thousand times. "What was her name?" she asked Emily.

"Diana Klugh."

"Oh, now I remember!" Ruby said. "She was the one who loved the Trinidad fairy tales and wouldn't let me stop telling them!"

"Yes, yes, yes!" Emily cried. "I can't tell you how blessed we are in this community to have you move here. You are the best doctor in the world, and we love you so much! Have you seen today's paper?"

Emily pulled out a small newspaper article, which had a picture of Ruby in her physician garb. It was titled: *Dr. Ruby moves to Middleville!*

I looked at Ruby to see how she was handling all this adoration. Fortunately, I couldn't tell if she was blushing on account of her beautiful, Trinidadian chocolate skin. Ruby was an introvert, so you'd never know what she felt unless she told you. But from the look I saw on her face, I'd say she certainly seemed to handle this flattery just fine.

"So, where can we find a small, comfortable, three-bedroom home?" I asked Emily, changing the subject.

"I thought I'd take you over to see the lake homes," she said.

We piled into Emily Watson's large SUV. It seemed that everyone in Middleville had a four-wheel-drive vehicle. Cars were certainly in the minority and for good reason. Only these huge contraptions could get people through the heavy winter snow and haul all of the hunting and fishing equipment that people used on a regular basis. One of the more interesting features of the town was the oversized, detached garages. It wasn't unusual to find someone with a six-acre plot of land that featured a garage that was larger than the house. Like most small towns, it seemed that people placed a higher priority on their tough, rugged hauling vehicles, than on the size of the physical spaces in which they lived.

As we drove slowly down Main Street, I noticed that downtown Middleville was a collection of maybe a dozen single-story buildings whose façades hid boxy, brick buildings. If it weren't for the fact that Main Street was tarred, it would look pretty much like a scene from an old western. Once beyond downtown, we turned off onto a dirt roadway. I had never imagined anywhere like this in my life. Houston was all I'd ever known, and compared to it, this was basically a bush! And driving at thirty miles an hour actually takes some getting used to, but once you start enjoying the trees and the natural, open spaces, you can actually begin to appreciate it.

"That's the Healy's old house over there," Emily said, pointing to a house to our left. "I can't show you that one because they died a few years back, and their stupid kids won't come up here and clean the place out. Some people just make me sick! And that's Kearney's farm over there. He is a pervert and a reckless womanizer, but he's rich. He owns almost all the rental houses in these parts, but with all the hooker babes he hangs out with, I can't bring myself to tell you what he does with it all. I wouldn't want to show you any of his places either."

Although I appreciated Emily's concern for us, I was beginning to get impatient with her gossiping. We just wanted a house, not a full report on everyone's business.

"Okay, here we go," she said. "This is Nancy Ohm's old house. She moved out when she married Pastor Donahue."

Ruby cut in. "Really? I didn't know Pastor Donahue got married."

"Yes," Emily said. "And boy, was it ever a scandal! It almost ripped his entire congregation apart when Nancy left her boyfriend of ten years and shacked up with the good pastor. But hey, I'll save you the details. After all, it's none of our business anyway, right?"

"Right!" I blurted out, unaware that I actually spoke out my thoughts.

Emily took us into the empty home, and we looked around. It had three bedrooms, lots of functional space, a basement, and a wonderful, breathtaking view of Middle Lake. We were hooked. I was especially fond of the fact that I could build myself a nice music-recording studio in the basement, and there was plenty of room for Junior to play. Ruby and I talked it over for a few minutes, and we agreed to make an offer on the spot. We'd had enough. We weren't looking for a dream home—just a place where we could start to rebuild.

"We'll take it," I said.

"Oh! Wonderful," Emily gushed. "I'll get papers drawn up for you immediately. You'll love this home. It's just far enough away from everyone that you'll have a lot of privacy, and close enough to the city, so that you can go in and out easily."

We hauled back into her SUV, and she asked us if we were planning on going to the parade that evening.

"We didn't know about it," I said.

"Oh, you have to go! Everyone will be there. It will be a great introduction for you, and you can hear everyone's juicy stories at the same time. I can take you there!"

Ruby and I nodded and looked to each other. Sure, why not?

We went back to Emily's office and signed all the real estate papers. She ran some numbers, called the bank, and got our mortgage information all taken care of. We were impressed with her speed and efficiency. No bottlenecks or long waits, just good old, small-town, first-name-basis relationships with all the people she needed to work with to get things done. Before long, it was official; we now lived in small-town USA. We piled back into her car, and she drove us to the park, where the parade was being held.

Once we got there, we began to replay the same scene over and over; one person or the other would come over to us and ask Ruby if she remembered the time she saved her from near death or helped with her hernia or personally watched over a sick child. Ruby was a veritable hero in these parts! Everyone had a story in which she had been heroic, kind, or just plain funny in her doctoring. It was a marvel to watch Ruby take all this in, when only a few days ago, she had been crying about how she thought she wasn't a good doctor. I was really happy for her! This is what she needed—a place where she was appreciated.

"Dr. Ruby!" boomed a voice from the crowd watching the parade. A large, heavyset gentleman strode over to us with a huge smile on his face. His greasy face and mustache told the story of a man who loved to have fun and who was kind and generous. His positive attitude was contagious. I liked this gentleman for some strange reason, even before I knew who he was.

"Now, you must be Dr. Ruby's husband," he said. "I'm Jake Donahue, director of purchasing at the hospital, and pastor of the Trinity Church!" He shook my hand with an incredibly strong grip.

"Hello," I beamed. "I'm Mike Jordan. Pleased to meet you." He had already moved on and grabbed my wife in a bear hug, lifting her completely off the ground. Emily stepped back, so that she wouldn't get run over. Thankfully, I was holding Junior.

"So glad you could move up here, Ruby!" he growled at her. "We've been hoping you'd make that decision for years!"

"We kinda had to at this point," Ruby said.

"Well, God works in strange ways sometimes. Everything for a reason!"

Pastor Donahue had a way of speaking with a smile on at all times, as though it were glued onto his face. He just radiated warmth, happiness, and joy. I couldn't imagine this man ever being sad. I just didn't think a frown could fit on that face of his. He spent the next thirty minutes or so, walking around with us, introducing us to the town folk. He also offered to drive us back to our hotel, which let Emily off the hook for the evening. Dana Watson, Emily's twin sister, came over to join us as we were eating some fried cheese curds with Pastor Donahue.

"So, you finally made the move?" Dana asked, looking at Ruby.

"Yep!"

"Why, we are so happy this has happened, right Emily?"

"Right." Emily said, beaming with joy.

"We will have to tell all the board members about this," Dana said. Turning to me as if to provide some background, she continued, "Emily and I are both members of the hospital board of directors now, and I think this needs to be celebrated!"

Pastor Donahue jumped in, "I'd go slow on that if I were you ladies. This is just a trial for Dr. Ruby. Let's not count our eggs before they're hatched."

Dana retreated with a temporary, disappointed look. Just then, she saw someone across the park and excused herself. "Come on, Emily, we have to go and hear the latest news about Sally's husband. I think this will be juicy!" And with that, they were gone.

"So, I see you've met our town gossips!" Pastor Donahue said. We laughed.

"Mike," he said, this time addressing me. "I heard that you're a leadership development consultant."

"Yes, I am, actually." I was surprised he had already heard, but I was happy to be addressed as myself for once, not just "Dr. Ruby's husband."

"I also heard you're a musician."

"Really?" How on earth had he heard about *that* part of my life?

"Absolutely. It's a small town! We know everything about you already!" he joked.

I didn't laugh.

"You ought to come visit with me at Trinity Church one of these days. We have a band there that could use musicians, and I think there would be a lot for us to talk about on the leadership side as well. Also, as a bonus, I can teach you how to fish when you visit."

Everyone always offered to teach visiting city folk how to fish or hunt. It seemed like a standard part of the stereotypical midwestern "nice" character.

"Thanks," I said. "I just might take you up on that."

Pastor Donahue dropped us off at our motel at about 7:00 P.M., after an exhausting afternoon at the parade. As we settled down in our room, Ruby and I talked about how this might actually be a great move after all. Middleville certainly wasn't the busy city life we were used to in Houston, but it had its benefits. Everyone knew your name, and people seemed to genuinely care and share a real sense of community here.

Ruby had to work the next morning. She made a list of things for me to do, including getting some things for Junior and taking him to the hospital at specific times for feeding. By all accounts, even though I'd be in our new home, it looked as though I was going to be just as busy as she was. We laid Junior down and retired to the motel bed. Before long, the phone rang, and Ruby pushed the speakerphone button. It was Pastor Donahue.

"Dr. Ruby, sorry to interrupt your evening! But you need to come in to the hospital right now. There has been an emergency!"

Ruby shuffled out of bed and ran for the door with the trained urgency of an emergency room physician. I sat up and watched her grab her stethoscope, throw on her white coat, and scurry away to her job. I had no idea what was going on. As she slammed the door and vanished into the night, I remember thinking, "Good-bye Houston. Hello, Middleville, USA."

The Hospital

The motel phone rang at about 3:00 A.M. It was Ruby.

"How are you doing, honey?" she asked.

"I'm good. But you're the one who had to rush out of here. How are *you* doing?"

"Oh, just ducky. But all hell broke loose here yesterday, which is why I'm here, and why your new LeaderPractice firm might have a consulting gig sooner than you think. Can you talk?"

"Absolutely!" I had no idea what she was talking about, but the consulting gig part sounded extremely interesting.

"Okay. Apparently there was a surprise visit last week by the Rural Hospital Commission, the RHC. That's the body that regulates and provides accreditation for hospitals like ours. When they visited, they marked the hospital down for not having met their minimum standards of performance in several areas. During their audit, they noticed that there was no medical director on staff, and that there was also no physician on call for trauma and emergency after hours. There was only a PA, a physician's assistant, on staff. One thing you should know is that a PA has to have a physician countersign everything, even if just nominally, and oversee his or her work. Apparently, ever since the last CEO left there has been chaos, and a leadership vacuum. People have been reluctant to do anything that is outside their job scope. Even physicians won't come in to the hospital in an emergency because it is 'not their job.' Basically, they had a situation here where no physician was around, and only a PA was on staff."

"Honey," I said. "How does this involve me as a consultant?"

"Hold on," she said. "I'm getting to it." Ruby had a thing for detail. I just wanted to get to the meat of the story.

"All right, now here's the tough part," she said. "Just yesterday evening, probably while we were at the park, a trauma patient with severe, complex injuries came into the hospital after a two-vehicle car crash. The PA did the best he could, but the driver died in the Emergency Room. In hindsight, no one should have died because the main injury, which could have been addressed, was somehow missed in the diagnosis. They called me in when the patient was coding, but when I got here, it was already too late."

"That's very sad," I said.

"Yes, and unfortunately that can happen sometimes, but here's where you come in. Pastor Donahue asked me to tell you that the RHC is coming in at some point tomorrow for a follow-up visit. The way things are, this could really hurt the organization. Pastor Donahue says that the board of directors already put out the word for anyone who can stand in as an interim CEO while they continue their search for a replacement, and when they heard you were a leadership consultant to major organizations, their eyes lit up. They need someone here to help address any personnel issues the RHC might have."

"I see," I said. "So, they need someone to dress up in a suit and talk smart about 'leadership issues'?"

"Yep."

"Why can't they get one of the existing leaders at the hospital to represent them to the RHC?"

The Three Gaps between Goals and Greatness

"I'm not sure. Maybe the RHC needs to know someone is dedicated solely to these particular administrative issues, and not to other jobs in the organization."

"What if I can't help them?"

"They could shut the hospital down."

"Okey-dokey!" I said, with a touch of irony. "I'll be there first thing in the morning."

"Great. I'll tell Pastor Donahue. My friend Brittany will take care of Junior while you're at the hospital. A patient's coming—gotta go."

Click.

At 7:00 A.M., I called Brittany and arranged to have her meet me at the hospital to pick up Junior for the day. I threw on my black suit and my red power tie, bundled up the baby, and headed out to the hospital.

The Middleville Hospital was built at the top of a hilly section of town. As I approached it, I could imagine the breathtaking views of Middle Lake that could probably be seen from the patient's windows. It was a one-story, all-brick building with a circular driveway in front. I parked in the visitors' area and headed toward the entrance. I walked into the hospital and immediately perceived the smell of medicine and antiseptic cleaning agents in the air. I marveled at how Ruby—or anyone for that matter—could endure the daily anguish of sick people, the constant sight of blood, and the smell of chemicals that permeated the air. Ruby and I had always joked at how we had two Dr. Jordans in the house, but only one of us was a "real" doctor. I had no stomach for blood or medicines, so I was glad to be a doctor of philosophy and not a "real" doctor!

The hospital's administrative assistant gave me a name badge and took me around the building for a quick tour and a meet and greet with the hospital's five team leaders. I was introduced to

Elizabeth Pierce, director of patient services; Pat D'Arcy, director of nursing services; Amy Wells, director of the business office, and good old Pastor Donahue, director of purchasing, who looked very different in the hospital environment with his white shirt and red tie. After meeting those four leaders, the administrative assistant informed me that Janet Knutson, the human resources director, was waiting for me in her office. I thanked her and walked toward the H.R. office.

"Come on in!" a female voice thundered through the door. I began to wonder if all Middleville people were this loud. For some reason, I mentally pictured the H.R. director to be just as large, tall, and endowed with the girth of pastor Donahue, the other thundering voice I'd heard around here. But I was wrong. When I opened the door, the woman with her hand outstretched was of medium height but extremely thin—almost paper-thin. I found myself wondering why she didn't tip over after bellowing out such a loud greeting. She motioned for me to take a seat.

"Dr. Jordan!" she announced, looking up at me. I thought the windows would break from the sheer volume of her voice.

"Please, call me Mike," I said.

"Excellent, Mike. I'm Janet Knutson, H.R. director of Middleville Hospital. Have a seat."

She had excellent elocution, and spoke in a very slow, purposeful drawl. Listening to her was almost a hypnotic experience. She had the kind of voice you'd hear narrating documentary movies on the History channel - very proper, very professional.

"Thank you, Ms. Knutson."

"Oh, please call me Janet."

"Fair enough," I said.

"You're probably wondering why you're here, aren't you?"

The Three Gaps between Goals and Greatness

I rolled my eyes and started to speak, but she continued too quickly for me to get a word in. I sat back and listened.

"The hospital board asked us to keep an eye out for an interim CEO or leadership consultant while they continue their search for a permanent CEO. So far, that search hasn't turned up anyone willing to live in a small town. And then it turns out that you and your wife happened to relocate to this area, and we couldn't resist the opportunity to make your acquaintance. By the way, your wife is an excellent doctor. One of the things we've learned here is that technical medical skills are not as important as people skills. Whenever a patient tells us they love one of our doctors, they never say, "Oh, what a great, technical EKG she did on me!" They always talk about the fact that the doctor cared or was a great teacher or something more about how she made them feel than anything else. Your wife really makes our patients feel great, and we're glad that she has decided to move up here."

"Thanks," I said, hoping to ask her a quick question, but she had already moved on to another part of her conversation. I held my question, kept quiet, and sat back again.

"Have you ever heard the saying, 'She's a good nurse, but …'?"

"No," I said.

"Well," she said. "That's one of the big problems we have here in our hospital. Behavior! The problem with people here isn't a lack of technical performance. The problem is character. Some people just have really bad behavior!"

"So, what do you do with people like that?" I asked.

"Fire 'em!" She spat, with a dramatic wave of her hand. "Just get 'em off the bus!"

I kept quiet after that, shocked by her arrogance and lack of tolerance. No wonder dysfunction was at a maximum here.

"If you are interested in working with us, you'll need to know a lot about the history of our team. Let me tell you a quick story about the hospital," she said and proceeded to run through various stories about the organization. I was at a loss for where her soliloquy was going until she said, "You see, we always put loyalty first, and we always think in terms of the team."

Finally, I managed to force myself into the conversation she was happily conducting with herself.

"Why is the Rural Health Commission's low grade on performance, efficiency, and productivity such an emergency?" I asked.

"Well, you've got to remember, we are a nonprofit hospital, so we're not measuring things like sales per se. What we measure are the kinds of reports and accreditation we get from the RHC and other regulators. What they say about us affects our financial reimbursement from the government. Without reimbursement, we'd have to shut down. Let me tell you a story about what happened when—"

"Wait, I have another quick question," I blurted out. I had finally figured out that the best way to get a word in edgewise was to jam it in right before the next story. "Despite what the RHC has said about performance issues, what do you think is really at the heart of the hospital's problems?"

"Oh, that's a great question," she said. "Really simple. The problem is our employees. They are lazy, unaccountable to anyone, only interested in collecting their paychecks, and they just don't seem to be motivated to get anything done. That's why we've got the RHC breathing down our backs."

I found her response extremely telling.

"I met some of your leadership team colleagues this morning. Tell me a little bit about how leadership has worked here in the absence of a CEO."

"Well, ever since the last CEO left, we've been kind of running around like headless chickens. I'd say that the employees don't really understand what is required of them. We've done our best to guide the donkeys to the stream, but obviously, we're unable to force them to drink, or else, performance would be much better around here."

"It looks like you've got a handle on the pulse of the people in the organization. May I ask you to do a quick thought exercise with me?"

"Absolutely!"

"Based on your observations, tell me one strength, and one weakness for each of the leaders on your team."

"Oh, that's easy! Pastor Donahue is basically Mr. Nice. He can't handle difficult employee issues because he isn't willing to disappoint anyone. But he's also the life of our leadership team. He keeps us positive whenever we're descending into the pits of negativity. Amy Wells from the business office is a very experienced finance person, and she's kind of like a big sister to everyone. However, she is overly critical and nitpicky. No one can stand her when she gets into one of her detail-oriented fits. Elizabeth is a complex one. I think her problem is just that she is not altogether there. She doesn't seem to pay attention to what's going on. Then there's Pat D'Arcy. Frankly, I wouldn't trust her if she were the last person on earth. She repeats whatever you tell her in confidence without fail. She's a good nurse, *but* ... her behavior sucks!"

She leaned back in her chair and breathed a heavy sigh, seemingly proud of her informal assessment. I took advantage of the break and jumped in.

"You forgot someone," I said.

"Who?"

"Yourself."

"Oh," she said, smiling and swiveling in her chair. "That's pretty simple. People see me as a firm, solid H.R. leader. I get things done, and I think we need that kind of steady hand around here."

"And what about any weaknesses you might have?" I asked.

"Well, occasionally people have said that I have a bad temper, and I'm a micromanager."

"So, what are you doing about this alleged temper and micromanaging style?"

"Nothing, really," she said.

"If I'm going to come on board to help your leadership team, I'll need a commitment from you. Can you promise me you'll try to address these issues in the next few days and weeks?"

"Sure," she said. "Why not?"

I could tell she was not very thrilled with this conversation, but she nonetheless seemed willing to cooperate. I leaned over and looked her squarely in the eyes.

"You know what I think the real problem at Middleville is?"

"What?"

"It's your leadership team," I said.

She looked at me for a minute, with an expression on her face like a deer in headlights.

"And why do you say that?"

"Because the quality of an organization's performance is directly proportional to the quality of its leaders."

"I love that!" she sputtered. "I love the way you said that! And it reminds me of something that happened a few years ago. Let me tell you a quick story about the CEO before our last CEO... you'll get the point in a minute."

I sat back in my chair and listened. Somehow I knew this was going to be a long morning.

Ninety Days

Ruby and I moved into our new home just three days after we first saw it. Our realtor, Emily Watson, was able to pull all kinds of strings to help us rent the home until our official closing day. Now that we were a bit more settled in, I had the luxury of unpacking my musical equipment, and setting up my recording studio in the basement. As I was working, I was reminded of Pastor Jake Donahue's offer to visit with him and potentially join his church band. But what I really wanted was to get his take on the performance problems at the hospital.

I called him on his cell phone, and he invited me over to his Church. As I drove over there, it occurred to me how driving at thirty miles an hour can change the things you notice as you drive by. It was a beautiful, sunny September afternoon in Middleville. When I finally arrived at the Trinity Church of Christ, I found it to be a quaint, all-brick affair nestled in a very wooded area of town. I parked in the side garage and let myself in.

"Hello Pastor Donahue," I said.

"Oh—call me Jake!" He thundered, smiling and waving for me to take a seat. "So, have you decided to come do your leadership development magic on us?"

"Well it depends, Jake. Tell me, why do you think that the HRC graded the hospital so low on performance, efficiency, and productivity?"

"To be honest with you, I haven't a clue!" He said.

I decided to get right to the point. "Jake, I know that things are going crazy over there at the hospital, and its easy to push blame all over the place, but I think that your leadership team is really where the work needs to be done."

"I can't argue with your there." He said.

"For one thing, I think your H.R. director is a piece of work. She just doesn't seem to listen to anyone but herself. And to be perfectly honest, from what I've heard so far, I think your leadership group could benefit from a team assessment to figure out how we might be able to help turn things around in the organization. I'm going to think seriously about consulting for you, but I can't make any promises right now."

"Hey—that's still better than the prognosis we had just last week. As you can imagine, it is hard to find talent out here. We're glad for any help we can get. And speaking of leadership," he said, "I should tell you that I've got my own struggles over here at Trinity Church. And I don't think I'm even one-tenth as uptight as Janet Knutson. In fact, some people would say I'm too *nice*. Can you imagine that? I've actually been accused of being too nice around here! And now, our Church board is threatening to go get a different pastor under the weak argument that they think I'm too busy to do both medicine and pastoring."

"That's too bad," I said.

"Can you help with some kind of leadership assessment here at the Church as well?"

"Sure. Maybe I can help give you an outside opinion on your leadership situation. Tell me a bit about the structure of your team here." I could feel my entrepreneurial, consultant hat sliding slowly into place.

"Actually, I'm glad you asked. I have an assistant pastor who is kind of like my vice president of everything, and then we have appointed volunteers from the parish that handle different things like the music directorship, the finances, and all the other tasks that need to be done. I answer to only God and the Church board, which is made up of ten elected parishioners."

"So, in a sense, you're the CEO here?" I asked.

"I guess you could say that."

"Tell me, Jake, how exactly is your *'nice'* problem affecting your leadership?"

"I guess the only thing I can say is that people don't take me seriously because I'm always nice, making jokes, and goofing around. I don't bark orders much, I guess."

"How is it affecting your leadership at the hospital?"

"Same thing. People say I'm just too nice."

"I'm willing to bet that's not the real problem. Nice is never a bad thing. I think we should look deeper into this, maybe even do a psychological assessment, and then talk further about steps that you can take to change whatever the problem really is. Are you willing to try something new?"

"Absolutely!" He said.

"Excellent. We'll talk some more about it," I said, moving on to the other reason I came to visit with him. "Where does your band setup?"

He took me over to the main church chamber where the band played. There were probably a thousand seats in his church, and it featured a nice, two-story interior elevation that I could only imagine would be acoustically marvelous. The musical instruments were tucked into a corner to the left of the stage. I sat on the church piano and ran through a few of my favorite jazz licks in the key of G minor.

"Impressive!" He thundered. "So, are you gonna join our band?"

Before I could answer, in walked Emily and Dana Watson, the town gossips.

"How'ya doin'?" sang Dana, obviously the more extroverted of the two. Pastor Donahue smiled at them. "Mike here was just about to treat me to a concert."

"Wow, so he's multi-talented? Isn't Dr. Ruby lucky?"

"Hi Dana, Hi Emily!" I said, ignoring her flattery.

"So, have you heard?" Dana asked, once she got closer to the musical section.

"Heard what?" Pastor Donahue asked. I stopped playing the piano and kept a respectfully puzzled look on my face.

"It looks like RHC has given the hospital board ninety days to do something about performance, or else they are going to shut it down."

"Ninety days? When did this happen?" Pastor Donahue said. "Weren't they supposed to come and visit at least one more time before they reached a final conclusion?"

"We just got the letter. They didn't even want to bother coming back. They heard what happened with that patient the other day. Basically, they just said that if we don't get some kind of leadership in here and clean up these problems, we can pretty much kiss having a hospital goodbye."

I looked at Pastor Donahue. He looked at me. We stood speechless. In my mind, all I could see was the town closing down, with hundreds of people losing their jobs and moving out. I imagined poor Pastor Donahue without a job or a parish. Emily and Dana would actually have nothing to gossip about for once. I didn't even want to think about what that might mean for Ruby and me. I stood up to leave.

"Well, I guess I should be going, Pastor Donahue."

"So, are you going to help us out with some leadership consulting?"

"We'll see," I said. "I think I might have an even better idea."

I said goodbye to Dana, Emily, and Pastor Donahue, and got back in to my car. As I drove out of the Trinity Church parking lot, I quickly dialed a number on my phone. A voice answered, thin and choppy across my weak cell phone signal.

"Ravi!" I said. "Where on earth are you now?"

"I'm in India, riding an elephant!" He said. "I'm following my bliss!"

"Congratulations," I said. "May I ask you a question?"

"Yes, my bush rat friend! Quickly, while this animal here stays steady!"

"Well, you've always told me you liked my audacity." I said.

"You got that right!"

"Well, I think I have another audacious idea for you."

"Oh boy! What is it this time, Mike?"

"How would you like to be an interim Hospital CEO?"

Pelè Raymond Ugboajah, PhD

The Leadership Team

To my absolute shock and amazement, Ravi accepted the challenge. My wife Ruby couldn't believe how I had managed to pull off such a coup. Essentially, I had engineered a way to turn my former CEO into my present CEO at a new organization! Neither of us was sure why Ravi accepted the offer. It was hard to know whether he decided he had had enough bliss in his journey, or if he wanted to add the cold Midwest to his bucket list of travel accomplishments. Whatever his reasons, he was willing to come out of his self-imposed retirement. He accepted my invitation, put in a call to members of the hospital board of directors and was offered the job of interim CEO. It was a no-brainer for the board; Ravi had an excellent track record of leadership as a CEO in both a leadership development firm and a for-profit hospital. Given the fact that not too many people were willing to relocate to Middleville, they were lucky to have him. Also, they were getting two seasoned experts at the same time—me as a leadership consultant, and Ravi as an interim CEO. The deal was too good for them to pass up, and within days, Ravi was on a plane from Bombay, India, to Middleville, USA.

Wasting no time at all on the very first day he arrived, he called a meeting of the entire leadership team to begin an introductory process. Everyone was in attendance: Pastor Donahue, Amy Wells,

Elizabeth Pierce, Pat D'Arcy, Janet Knutson, and me. I was overjoyed. It was almost like the good old days back at LeaderTraits, only this time, we were in the middle of nowhere, and we had only ninety days to turn an entire organization around.

"My name is Ravi," he said, speaking from the head of the boardroom table. "I've accepted the position of interim CEO here at Middleville Hospital. You've already met my partner in crime here, Dr. Mike Jordan." The group nodded in my direction. "Upfront, I want you to know that over the next ninety days, Mike will play the role of PhD guru, and I'm going to be the chief sales guy. That means that he is going to be rolling out a specific program we've discussed in the past, called LeaderPractice, and it will represent our best chance to correct the downward course the hospital is currently on. My job over the next ninety days is to work with each of you to sell that program to the entire employee base. Any questions?"

No one had any questions. Internally, I had a huge question, but this wasn't the right forum to bring it up. I wondered how Ravi had gone from doubting my ideas to giving me such a powerful introductory platform. However, the more he spoke, the more I realized why he had accepted this interim CEO offer in the first place: it seemed more and more that he wanted to give me a chance to prove that LeaderPractice worked—and he wanted to be here to see it himself.

"I'm going to get straight to the issue here," he said. "This morning I had a chance to walk around and learn the local vernacular, including great words like uff dah, you betcha, and yah sure."

We laughed. Ravi definitely had a sense of humor.

"On a more serious note, I've been told that we have a very experienced leadership group. I've also been told we have great, talented employees, although there seems to be something amiss at the moment. We have the very best medical technology, and plenty of money in the bank. Yet, despite these apparent advantages, the Rural Hospital Commission has marked us for extinction. Can anyone—other than Mike—tell me why?"

Predictably, Janet Knutson jumped in. "I think it's the employees. As the RHC has said, they just aren't performing to the best of their potential. What we have here is a performance, efficiency, and productivity problem."

"Does anyone here disagree with Janet's viewpoint?"

No one spoke.

"That's too bad," he said. "Not only do I encourage vigorous debate on this team, I was actually hoping someone would disagree. You see, from everything Mike and I have seen as leadership consultants, we know that the fish usually stinks from the head down. I believe that the problems we have here at the hospital are not just procedural and performance issues—regardless of what the RHC has diagnosed. I think the problems are all behavioral, people issues, and they start with us, the leadership team, and they work their way down. We have no hope of fixing anything in the organization if we don't fix the leadership first. What are your thoughts about that?"

Everyone nodded. Besides Janet Knutson, this was not a very vocal group of leaders.

"All right, before we adjourn today, I'm going to ask for one more thing from each of you. During this process, I will need your complete participation. I want you to confront ideas openly and be fearless. I am not here to give anyone a hard time. We are a team. We need trust, openness, and the ability to engage in constructive debates over how things should be done. I don't want myself and our friend Ms. Knutson here to be the only ones talking."

The group chuckled.

Pelè Raymond Ugboajah, PhD

"Okay. Let's get to work. First thing tomorrow, I'd like to have our first planning meeting. At that time we will go over the LeaderPractice model." He looked over to me, seemingly for the first time. "Mike, are you ready to teach us the model?"

"Absolutely, Ravi," I said, overjoyed that my friend and mentor was in charge. "You betcha!"

The Idea

Our planning meeting started promptly the next day at 8:00 A.M. Ravi opened the meeting and asked me to jump right in and explain the LeaderPractice model.

"Thanks, Ravi," I said. "Before we get started, I'd like to reiterate what Ravi said yesterday, which is a statement that is really at the heart of everything you'll hear and see this morning. The facts as we've discovered them are as follows. We are an organization with many talented employees. We have solid managers and directors with extensive resumes, and an executive team of hardworking leaders with proven expertise. We also have the infrastructure, the money, and the collective organizational experience to achieve pretty much any goal we want with healthcare in this community. Yet, we have low performance, low morale, low productivity, and now, we have only ninety days to fix all of this, or our organization will be shut down. That's what we see here. Does anyone disagree with that analysis?"

Silence. Even Janet Knutson kept quiet.

"Okay. In that case, I'll launch into what we think the solution is. I think we all agree that *people* are at the core of our solution, but you'll find that there are two important and distinct aspects that determine how our people will help us implement our solution—their performance and their behavior. First, let me tell you about a popular business concept known as the *execution gap*. Basically, what this term means is that there is a wide divide between great goals and organizational greatness. The simple fact here is that organizations become great because they actually get great things done and not simply because they set great goals. Not closing this execution gap can result in significant financial or value losses in an organization. But our real question is not whether an execution gap exists here at the hospital because we know that it does. The real challenge we have is to understand the true nature of that gap, so that we can become smart enough to close it."

I could see that I had everyone's attention now. I walked over to the white board and asked Ravi if I could create some visuals for them. He nodded his approval, so I began with a table explaining the driving ideas behind conventional wisdom, and how that differs from the LeaderPractice approach.

Model	Driving Idea
Old	Execution = Better [**Performance**]
New	**Performance** = Better [Behavior + Habits + Community]

"The execution gap that most people talk about is way too big and ambiguous for our purposes. Most people think the best way to close the execution gap is by improving performance. Based on my research and experience, I've found that better performance is only possible if three other gaps are filled. Those gaps are behavior, habits, and community, and they are actually the essential building blocks to organizational performance, yet most organizations either ignore them or pay them lip service. Since behavior, habits, and community are the building blocks of better performance, in reality, this is what the execution gap really should look like:

The Execution Gap = [Behavior Gap + Habits Gap + Community Gap]

"For example, let's talk about the behavior gap. This first gap occurs when leaders and their employees are too busy working on quantifiable performance measures—which is what they are compensated against. However, at the same time, they never pay much attention to their own individual or team behavior, which ironically, has the power to either support or derail their performance in the long run. Because people aren't overtly compensated against behavior, there is really no strong incentive to modify behavior for the greater good of the organization. Despite this overwhelming focus on performance, it is behavior that can bring down the best-laid plans, teams, leaders, and organizations. So here's a quick question for you—why is it that people only tend to focus on measuring and improving performance, while seemingly ignoring behavior?"

Amy Wells jumped in. She had a very open spirit toward learning. "I think our people are just too busy with their real work. They just think that managing behavior is not their job, and they'd rather leave that to H.R."

Janet Kuntson rolled her eyes, as though demonstrating agreement with Amy about the troubles her H.R. team had had to endure.

"Exactly!" I said. "The main reason people ignore behavior is that they are just too busy with *work*. They consider the one thing that they are measured and paid against—their performance—to be the only thing worth addressing. But in a sneaky sort of way, their behavior, and the behavior of others around them, conspires to derail their efficiency and productivity."

Ravi jumped in. "This is like the parable of the chicken and the egg. Think of a chicken that is producing great eggs. It's kind of like trying to protect the eggs, which are the end product, while starving the chicken. What will happen is that eventually, the chicken will die of hunger, and then you'd have no more eggs. We have to feed the chicken if we want to continue having great eggs."

I could see that Ravi's parable really hit home. Heads were nodding.

"By the way," I said. "I forgot to mention that if you ever need a parable, Ravi is our wisdom guru!"

There was a collective chuckle from the group.

"Okay, now let's talk about habits. The second gap is the habits gap, which occurs when organizations do not invest the time to help their employees turn behavioral skills and goals into habits—the one competency that is most important for predictable execution. When people don't repetitively practice the behaviors that contribute to the overall success of the organization, they can never improve on them, and they will always revert back to destructive comfort zone behaviors."

I looked around at each of them before asking my next series of questions, which I knew might cause an uproar.

"How many of you here have ever practiced a skill, like riding a bike or typing or playing the piano?"

Everyone raised a hand except Ravi. I picked Pastor Donahue.

"Okay. Pastor Donahue, can you give us an example of something you practiced, and what the results were?"

"Sure," he said, his smile filling the room. "I once practiced shooting. At first, I was lousy—always hitting anything but the target. Happily, no one was killed in my efforts."

We laughed.

"After doing it over and over, I very quickly became an expert. Now, there's pretty much nothing I can't hit, even if it's moving fast and is far away." He was visibly proud of his accomplishment.

"Excellent," I said. "Now, let's talk about behavior. Pastor Donahue, what one behavior do you think you could improve to make you a stronger contributor to our organization?"

"I'm too nice!" he growled.

Everyone laughed. At least he knew his own problem well.

"Great," I said. "That was very honest of you. Now, how many times have you *practiced* not being so nice?"

Silence.

"Have you ever practiced it? Even once?"

"Nope."

"Okay. That makes the point. I don't mean to pick on you, Pastor Donahue, but the fact is, like anything else, we can't expect to ever improve on behavior if we don't practice it. We all know that—especially in a service industry like healthcare—behavior is at the heart of most of our leadership and productivity issues. It would therefore make sense to practice specific, identified behaviors until they become habits."

I could see heads nodding at this point. Even Elizabeth Pierce, who had been quiet most of the morning, had a warm, knowing look on her face. I could tell this stuff was beginning to click for her.

"And finally, here's the third gap," I said, pointing to the third part of the equation. "The third gap is the community gap, which occurs when individuals and teams in organizations are too busy with their daily work to take advantage of how communities of practice can help to create lasting behavioral change. Although there is clear value in individual effort, human beings are social by nature, and it is through social interactions such as accountability,

Pelè Raymond Ugboajah, PhD

recognition, feedback, and mentorship that lasting behavioral growth can occur."

I erased the equation I had written on the wall and asked if anyone could give me an example of a community of practice of which they were aware where people came together under one purpose and helped each other get better. Everyone had a response. Elizabeth suggested her knitting group. Amy suggested her weight-loss group. Pastor Donahue suggested his church, and even Ravi suggested a jazz band. Everyone got the point.

"So, since we are all aware of the benefits of community, why is it that organizations create teams to address all kinds of tangible goals and projects but never to address employee behavioral growth?

Silence.

"Exactly!" I said. This is the big gap. And if you remember the three gaps I described, they all point at one common enemy—the perception that people have that they are just too busy with their "real" work to make time for managing, practicing, and growing behavior in the organization."

At that point, I went back to the board and drew the following diagram:

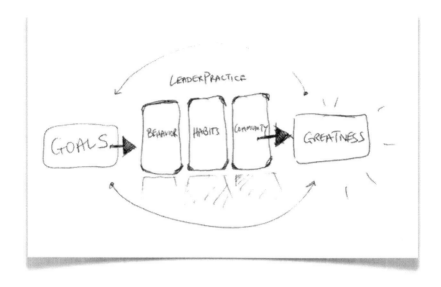

"Ladies and gentlemen, the plan that Ravi has asked me to share with you is something we call LeaderPractice—how to bridge the execution gap between our goals and our greatness. It will feature a series of weekly meetings throughout the organization over the next ninety days. Essentially, we will review our goals and address them both from a performance vantage point and a behavioral one, thus beginning to close the behavior gap right there. Next, we will assess our leaders, our teams, and the organization as a whole to identify specific behaviors on which we need to focus. Following that, we will practice improving or decreasing certain behaviors, based on what our assessments tell us, until our behavioral goals are automated and become habits. Essentially, we will practice until we create new habits that will drive our efficiency and productivity. Once our desired behavioral habits are in place, we will start to see that our performance goals will fall in place as well. By hosting weekly meetings structured in accordance with the three gaps, we will address the most critical behaviors that we need to improve. The meetings themselves will represent the community of practice component, and it is my belief that at the end of this process, we will begin to see not only results, but organizational greatness as well. The output of those results will simply revert back into inputs for another round of LeaderPractice goal-setting and execution processes. This is how we will bridge the gap between goals and greatness. Any questions?"

Ravi raised his hand. "Mike, can you show us where performance appraisals and psychological assessments fit into that model?"

I went back to the whiteboard and first pointed to the 'goals' box. "This is where performance goals are tracked." I then pointed to the 'behavior' box. "And this is where the psychological assessments are tracked. The only difference is that, instead of assessing, monitoring, and measuring them independently of each other—as is the norm—we will be aligning them and working on them together."

"Great job," Ravi said. "I'd like you to go ahead and get started rolling this out, and I want to see weekly follow-up reports. Ninety days will go by in a flash!"

From what I could see, heads were nodding in agreement. The meeting had gone very well. The one thing I didn't notice was the look of frustration on Janet Knutson's face.

The Ostrich Card

The first week was the most grueling of all. We wasted no time getting started. Ravi had to find a place to rent, so I put him in touch with realtor Emily Watson, who was more than happy to find him a place, as well as to provide her best recitation of the latest Middleville gossip. Back at the hospital, we sent out the first of two anonymous patient-satisfaction and employee-engagement surveys that we intended to use during the next ninety days.

The survey results we got back were predictable. On the one hand, patients felt that they appreciated certain individual doctors and nurses but found the hospital's overall service and reputation to be extremely poor. We certainly were not a hospital that they had a lot of confidence in. On the other hand, Middleville Hospital employees reported back to us that they were disengaged from their work, suffering from low morale, distrusted the leadership team, worked in an environment of fear for their jobs, and cared more about getting paid than actually producing success for the organization. In short, we found out what we knew already: externally, patients were not terribly excited by coming to our hospital, and internally, our organization was operating at the height of leadership and operational dysfunction.

Pelè Raymond Ugboajah, PhD

After receiving this first round of assessment results, Ravi and I held a series of meetings to determine what exactly would be the driving goals for the organization over the next ninety days. How would we measure our effectiveness from one week to the next? To address this question, we decided to create our first LeaderPractice Dashboard, a software spreadsheet that would help us assess the organization weekly, based on both performance and behavioral measures. Knowing that we would have to start our weekly LeaderPractice meetings at the leadership team level, we began by asking each member of the leadership team to take online psychometric evaluation tests, and 360-degree feedback evaluations from the employee base. After we got all our results back, we put them into the LeaderPractice Dashboard under the following headings:

PERFORMANCE MEASURES	BEHAVIORAL MEASURES
Service Effectiveness (from patient surveys)	Leadership Behavior Effectiveness (from 360-Degree Feedback and Psychometric evaluations)
Goal Effectiveness (from Employee Performance Reports).	Employee Engagement Surveys (for all employees)

The first feature of our LeaderPractice Dashboard spreadsheet was that all goals in the organization must be aligned and cascade from the top down. We did not want anyone working on any goal in the organization that wasn't somehow linked to the highest goals at the CEO level. The second feature was that all goals assigned to a leader or an employee had to have a physical, measurable performance component, as well as an associated, measurable behavioral component that would contribute to the success of that performance goal. In short, we were tying behavioral goals to performance goals in a very tight, coupled way; this was something that we had never done before, but which made absolute sense. We figured that this was our best opportunity to put a process in place that showed us the measurable effect of behavior on performance, as opposed to relegating behavior to the Darwinian free market and hoping for the best.

The process also called for Ravi to establish the very top CEO goals of the organization, from which we would work our way down, cascading and aligning all goals throughout the hospital until we got down to the daily tasks and behaviors of nurses, administrative assistants, and ward clerks. This way, everyone was working toward the exact same goals for both performance and behavior.

Finally, we had to sit down with the leadership team to gain buy-in for our top performance and behavioral goals, in preparation for an eventual, structured training and rollout to the entire organization. Ravi proposed an offsite lunch meeting for this particular process and invited the entire leadership team for the event. We chose the Big Bear Restaurant, one of two fine places to dine in Middleville; it was deep within the valley and right at the edge of Middle Lake. After everyone had exchanged light jokes and pleasantries, Ravi moved into the business of the day.

"Our purpose today is to prepare for the LeaderPractice weekly meetings by creating our first master list of performance and behavior goals." Ravi walked over to the chalkboard provided by the restaurant and drew a two-column table. On the left side, he wrote performance and on the right side, he wrote behavior.

"Okay, let's do some brainstorming. Remember, everything starts with our leadership group here. If we can get the LeaderPractice process right at our level, then we can expect success when rolling it out to the employee base. What are the top three performance goals that we want to drive this organization over the next ninety days, and how will we measure them?"

Pastor Donahue jumped in. "The first goal should be that we get a favorable review from RHC."

"Excellent," Ravi said, and wrote it on the board. "Measuring that would be simple. They either close us down or they don't, right?"

We laughed, albeit nervously.

"Any other goals?"

"The second goal," Pat D'Arcy said, "should be a 90% patient satisfaction score."

"Perfect!" Ravi said, and he wrote that down as well. "Next?"

"The third goal," Elizabeth Pierce said, "should be at least a 70% employee engagement score."

"Thanks, Elizabeth," Ravi said. "We can massage these numbers as needed, but at least, now we have these three top-level performance goals for the next ninety days. Let's call these the top CEO-level goals. Now, starting with this leadership team, we'll need to identify subordinate goals that will achieve these CEO goals, and then we need to also identify what supporting behaviors must be displayed by the person working on those goals. So, let's identify the top three behaviors that we want to promote or discourage over the next ninety days. Any ideas?"

"No micromanaging!" Pat D'Arcy said with a big grin on her face, staring straight at Janet Knutson. Janet did not smile back. I don't think she found that to be very funny.

Ravi wrote on the board and asked, "So, how will we measure micromanaging?'

I jumped into the conversation. "We can use either 180-degree or 360-degree feedback reports to measure this and all the other behavioral goals. As part of the weekly LeaderPractice meetings, every participant will bring along an individual LeaderPractice profile sheet where their performance and behavioral measures will be tracked and recorded. I'll talk about that later, after we get started on the structure and process of the weekly meetings."

"Thanks, Mike," Ravi said, writing down the first behavior. "Any other ideas?"

"Accountability," Elizabeth offered.

"Excellent," Ravi said. "And the third?"

"Trust!" Amy Wells blurted out.

"Perfect," said Ravi. "Now, Mike, can you walk us through the next steps in the process?"

I stood up and walked over to the board and sketched out what we had so far:

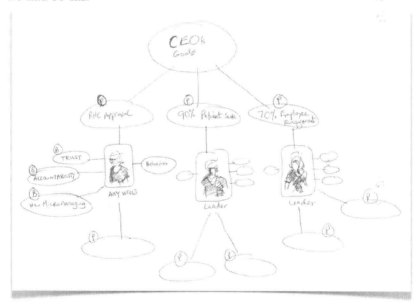

"So far," I said, "we have talked about the general performance and behavior goals we want to track and measure at the top level." I pointed to the three goals right under the CEO. "Our next step is to connect these three performance and behavior goals to specific leaders. Once a leader is assigned to a specific task, that leader will also become responsible for showing an improvement in the behavioral goals we've identified, as well as the performance goals for that task. For example, look at Amy Wells on the left side of that diagram. Assuming she is tasked with working toward the RHC approval goal, her performance will be affected by how well she addresses the three top behaviors we've identified at the organizational level, as well as one or two individual behavioral goals that are unique to her. The combination of general performance goals, job-specific performance goals, general behavior goals, and individual-specific behavioral goals will become her individual LeaderPractice profile, which will be the bases of her participation in our weekly LeaderPractice meetings." I then drew another diagram for what Amy Well's individual LeaderPractice Profile might look like:

"What you see here is essentially a profile for each individual. We can call it something like a LeaderPractice individual profile or something to that effect. Any questions?"

Janet raised her hands. "This looks like a whole lot of work! How will all this be measured? Who will make the time to be performing all of these 360-degree assessments to feed the weekly results? Frankly, I think this is a waste of time. We are a mission-critical hospital. We don't have time for all of this!"

"Janet," I said. "Thank you so much for such a powerful set of observations!" Looking at the rest of the group, I could see that they shared Janet's concerns to varying degrees, despite her harsh presentation of them. Even Ravi had an expectant look on his face. I think he was very interested in my answer as well. How would we be able to describe and sell these ideas for monitoring behavior to an already over-worked, stressed-out, demoralized employee population? Ravi stood up before I could respond.

"Janet raises a great point. This is really the most important issue of all," Ravi said. "The profile is fine, but I would really like for us to give it a better name. Naming your enemy is one of the best ways to begin a comprehensive attack. You cannot address what you don't know. Let's brainstorm for a name to describe this concept of "busy-ness" or this "more important work" stuff, which Janet refers to, which always makes us push behavioral issues to the side. And then, whatever name we come up with, let's use it as the description for this LeaderPractice profile, so that, as we roll this out, people are always reminded of the importance of doing this. What shall we call this profile?"

"The work-monster profile?" Amy offered, giggling.

"How about the unseen enemy profile'?" someone else said.

"The twilight zone profile?"

"Not seeing the forest for the trees?"

"How about the parable of the ostrich?" I said. Everyone turned to me with curiosity on their faces. "The problem here is the natural human tendency to focus on what we think is most important, while ignoring the rest of reality. For example, I have had this discussion many times with my wife, Dr. Ruby, and there are many ways we could describe it. Her favorite way of talking about it is in medical terms. She has this sarcastic joke that her friends all used to share back in their medical school days. It was about what happens when you ask a bunch of surgeons how a surgery went, and they reply, "Great surgery, but the patient died!" Obviously, they did all things right, but didn't actually do the right thing because other factors were present and conspired to bring about the patient's demise. This is the same concept we see in the parable of the ostrich who, in response to a coming danger, buries its head in the sand, erroneously imagining that the rest of its body is also concealed from that danger. When we focus exclusively on our "busy-ness" and "more important work," and ignore these behavioral, people issues, we are acting like the ostrich, foolishly ignoring the problem, and hoping it will vanish by itself."

"I love that!" exclaimed Ravi. "Let's use the ostrich parable to sell this thing. From now on, whenever we talk about wanting to do our "real work" and not wanting to invest time and energy into practicing our leadership and behavior at a LeaderPractice meeting, let's realize that we're displaying the foolishness of the ostrich. Everyone got that?"

We all nodded.

"I hate to be a spoiler," Janet Knutson said. "But I still don't see the value of having people trying to keep track of complex psychological and behavioral analyses during their busy workdays. Again, this is a hospital, folks, and we have less than ninety days to show some results! We really don't have time for games!"

The mood in the room descended from warm and fuzzy into a deep, dark chill. Janet certainly had a talent for punching holes in a positive situation.

"I have an idea," said Pastor Donahue. "Why don't we take that psychological data, boil it down to the three most significant attributes, and put them on a card. We could call it the ostrich card, and everyone could carry one with them in their pockets all day as a reminder."

"Brilliant!" Exclaimed Ravi. "Now that's what I call participation! Mike? Did you write that down? I think that's your signature idea right there. Everyone gets an ostrich card, and just like a business card, you carry it with you all day. That way, as situations arise, you can simply look at your card, remember your natural behavior tendencies, and compensate as needed."

"What a wonderful idea, Jake!" I said, and noticed the other leaders nodding their heads in agreement. Pat and Amy were all smiles, and even Elizabeth carried a warm smile as she rocked back and forth in her seat. Janet, however, was not smiling. She had a fierce look on her face.

"I think I'm going to owe you royalties for that one!" I said.

Pastor Jake Donahue laughed. "Just pay me back by joining my church band!"

"Excellent," Ravi said. "This is all coming together very well. Let's carry our ostrich cards with us and bring them to LeaderPractice meetings, so that we can work on not being like the foolish ostrich who gets eaten by a lion while hiding his head in the sand. By the way, Mike and I saw this happen at Enron. I wonder if the people at Enron had carried ostrich cards, would they have behaved so terribly in that organization? On that note, Mike, I want to see how this thing plays out at this leadership level first. When can we start the first LeaderPractice weekly meeting?"

Pelè Raymond Ugboajah, PhD

"We can start next week after I've worked with everyone to fill out their individual LeaderPractice profiles."

"You mean, ostrich cards, right?"

"Right!" I said, smiling and realizing my mistake.

"Great! The meeting is adjourned," said Ravi, addressing the entire group. "But I have one more request before you leave."

We all turned around and waited for his closing words.

"I'd like to ask each of you over to my apartment this Saturday at 5:00 P.M. for jazz band practice."

I found his invitation extremely interesting. Ravi and I didn't even know if anyone else played musical instruments.

"Does anyone here play musical instruments?" I asked.

"Doesn't matter," Ravi jumped in, grinning from ear to ear with his trademark smile. "Everyone must come. We're going to take some time off from practicing Leadership to practicing music. Mike, I need you to arrive at 4:30 P.M. so that we can get set up. And everyone, I need you to bring your ostrich cards with you. This is not a democracy, folks—this is an order!"

Well! I guess that was that. We all had smiles on our faces as we left the boardroom.

I think there was a general, positive feeling in that room as we left. Ravi was a good boss.

Jazz Practice

A arrived at Ravi's apartment at about 4:25 P.M. He lived in a heavily wooded part of town, near the end of Campbell Road. You could hardly call his place an apartment. It was more like a luxury condominium, nestled between tall evergreen trees, and hugging some steep rocks that jutted dangerously out of Middle Lake. The view from his backyard was spectacular—all lake, all sky. Ravi, ever the gentleman, greeted me at the door with a poetic observation of the world's beauty.

"My dear Dr. Mike Jordan," he said. "Is the day not simply heaven sent?"

"It really is," I said. "And you're in a great mood. What's the plan?"

"Well," Ravi said, inviting me to take a seat in his living room. "We need to do a little trust-building with the team. I want you to lead us in a process that will reveal our individual strengths and vulnerabilities. Remember how we would discuss psychometric results with LeaderTraits coaching clients, sometimes in group settings? That's what we're going to do today."

I nodded, and looking out onto his deck, I could see he had the entire band setup fully prepared and ready to go. The drums were set up, and the guitar and keyboards were all plugged in. He even had an amplified Bose speaker and mixing system all wired up and ready to go.

"I thought you wanted me to come early to help get the musical instruments set up?"

"I actually wanted you to come a bit earlier for another reason. I wanted to be able to spend some time to answer your burning question."

"And what question is that, Ravi?"

"Why I decided to accept your invitation to work in this interim CEO position."

I had to admit, that *was* a burning question for me, even though I wasn't complaining.

"I thought you accepted it because you admire my audacity," I joked.

"Well, that's close but not quite true." Ravi grabbed a beer from his fridge, and motioned for me to take one as well. "The real truth has to do with my personal journey to find my bliss."

We both sat down, and he continued.

"You see, after I retired, I traveled a bit and finally made my way to India. I went to see a guru to find out the meaning and direction of my life, and the true nature of the bliss I was seeking."

I wasn't sure if he was setting up a joke, or about to tell me one of his ancient parables, but I paid attention.

"I told the guru that I had lived a long and successful life making money for large corporations and that I just wanted to do something for myself for once. The kids had all moved on, and my wife and I were, frankly, living separate lives. Believe it or not, now that I had reached my sixties, I actually needed someone to tell me what the hell was next."

"And what did he say?" I asked, now realizing that Ravi was very serious.

"He said I needed to stop being so selfish!"

"Really?"

"Yes! And then he repeated the old saying: *If you save one life, you have saved the world.* He was trying to tell me that I had spent my life being a getter and that from now on, true bliss for me lay in becoming a giver. He told me to stop trying to achieve big things and just try to find one life to help, just one small thing to do for someone other than myself."

I commiserated fully with his story. In all honesty, for as long as I could remember, I had lived a life of intense focus on my own material needs and worries. Very seldom did I do things out of any kind of altruism. Life had always been about how to address my own issues, mitigate my own pain, and travel my own journey.

"And then what happened?"

"Then you called me for like the fifteenth time!" Ravi said, rolling his eyes. "That was when I realized that you, with your little idea about practicing behavior in organizations, were the life I was supposed to save. You were the bush rat I had to save from the rainy land of the lizards!"

"Wow," I said, with a touch of sarcasm. "Who knew our little idea was blessed all the way from India!"

"Well," said Ravi, "This LeaderPractice thing might be a little idea for you, but the more I learn about it, the more I see it as something that needs to be shared all over the world. People really need to practice behavior! They can't just wake up in the morning and expect that their personalities will magically work in the complex organizational cultures they find themselves in. Great athletes work hard to achieve excellence. Great motivational speakers are made, not born. Great leaders aren't born either, no matter what people say in the nature-versus-nurture debates. The fact is, anything that you want to do well must be given time, attention, and practice, and there is no reason why behavior should be any different in organizations. I really think you've got something here, Mike. I really do."

"Well," I said. "I guess I have some guru in India to thank for helping you see the light!"

We laughed, and then the doorbell rang. It was Elizabeth and Amy. They had decided to carpool together. Right behind them was Pat D'Arcy.

"Come on in!" Ravi exclaimed. Everyone filed in, hung up their coats, and took seats. Before long, Pastor Donahue and Janet Knutson showed up, and we had a full house.

"Thanks so much for coming over, everyone." Ravi stood up and asked us to follow him out onto his deck, where we could see his musical instruments set up, majestically framed by the breathtaking view of Middle Lake behind them.

"Today," Ravi said, "I'd like us to do two things. First, I'd like us to discuss our psychometric evaluations openly. And then after that, I'd like us all to play some jazz!"

"Ravi," Amy said. "I've never, ever played a musical instrument in my life!"

"Perfect!" Said Ravi. "Anyone else with less experience? The less musical talent you have today, the better!"

That sealed it. We were certainly going to be in for a treat. I had no idea what to expect. We filed back into the living room and began the discussions about our psychometric results.

"Mike, would you lead us in this discussion, please?"

"Certainly, Ravi," I said, and began to address the rest of the team. "Let me go first, so that you get a sense of the format and purpose of our discussion." I pulled out my ostrich card and first addressed my strengths.

"Okay, the first thing you should know is that these results are neither right nor wrong. They simply reflect what population of people my answers are closest to. They should be taken as a guide for further introspection and discussion not as gospel. My results say that I am strong in the following areas: interpersonal sensitivity and learning. This makes sense because I believe I am in fact easygoing and consider others' opinions seriously. I also know that learning for me is a life-long pursuit to which I am extremely drawn. My challenges are as follows: I am excitable, skeptical, and dutiful. I would have to agree here, as well, because I do tend to get excited by ideas, I do have a problem trusting at first sight, and frankly, I do sometimes aim to please others too much. Now we know how my personality shows up in this report. But personality is not the same as behavior! If personality is what I *am*, then behavior is what I *do*. My challenge is to practice my way out of destructive behaviors, especially when I'm under stress, so that these weaknesses I have don't turn into career or relationship destroyers. Also, my other challenge is to practice and grow my strengths. I think this is what we all have to do when we think of LeaderPractice. We have to first know our personality through psychometric instruments, 360-degree evaluations and the like, and then carefully build a plan with supporting parties to make sure not to allow behaviors to get in the way of organizational goals. Everyone got the format?"

People nodded.

"Great. Who wants to go next? Elizabeth?"

There was a look on Elizabeth's face that I had not seen before.

"To be perfectly honest, I'm really not comfortable doing this."

"Why is that?" I asked.

"Well, I kind of agree with Janet. I just don't see what this has to do with our healthcare work."

I noticed that, with the exception of Ravi and Dr. Donahue, the others were avoiding eye contact with me.

"Okay," I said. "Let's discuss that. Tell me, when you come to work, do you leave your personality at home?"

"No."

"Well then, when you interact with others, do they leave their behavior at home?"

"No, but I still don't see why I have to recite my strengths and weaknesses to you in this forum." I could see that Elizabeth was becoming increasingly uncomfortable with this process.

"All right," Ravi jumped in. "Let's return to this process after I show you a different viewpoint. Everyone, please, follow me to the musical instruments over here, and let's play some jazz."

We all filed over to Ravi's deck. You could almost touch the palpable sigh of relief that had suddenly filled the air. We got out on to the deck, and Ravi grabbed a guitar. From what I remembered him telling me, he could play pretty much any instrument he wanted, just like me. We were both fans of musicians like Stevie Wonder and Prince, who were versatile on any instrument. I admired the way he grabbed that guitar and started jamming.

"Now," Ravi said, jamming out some chords in the key of C, "I want you, Jake, to grab the drums, and play along with me."

Pastor Jake Donahue had an incredulous look on his face, but ever the sport, he jumped on the drums and started banging on the snare, completely out of step with Ravi. It was a disaster.

"Excellent," Ravi screamed above the awful cacophony of sounds coming from the drums. "Now, Amy, I want you to start playing that bass guitar over there. Go ahead, pick it up, and start playing it!"

Amy, smiling from ear to ear, took the challenge and picked up the bass guitar and started trying her best to outdo Pastor Donahue's outrageous drumming. All this time, Ravi kept a nice, solid chord progression going in the key of C major, regardless of what the other two instruments were doing.

"Okay," he said, "Now, Janet, Pat, and Elizabeth, please grab an instrument each. I have the baby grand piano over there, the acoustic guitar over there, and the Electric Fender Rhodes keyboard over here. Just join us and play along. We are in the key of C major!"

They all obliged, and at this point, I had to put my hands over my ears and bend over in pain. The one good thing here was that everyone was having a great time! All of a sudden, as quickly as he started, Ravi stopped, and motioned for everyone to stop.

"Thank you, ladies and gentlemen," he said. "Please leave your instruments, and return to your seats. Now, let me show you another side of jazz practice. Mike, please come over here and grab an instrument, and play along with me in C major."

I sat on the bench and began playing the Fender Rhodes piano, which was by far my favorite instrument. I was amazed that he had one. Ravi started his chord progression again in C-major. It was a simple I—IV—V progression, slightly funky, moving from C to F and then to G. I first started by finding his timing and structural placement of the chords, and then I played a subtle note-by-note rendition of the A-minor scale, the relative minor of C-major. Once I was sure of his progression, I started playing more notes, changing octaves, doing more adventurous runs and licks, and even switching from the relative A-minor scale to certain bluesy notes outside the scale. Before long, we were jamming like we had been doing this together for years. I then switched and started playing the chords while Ravi, sensing my move, started playing a blistering, weeping blues solo on top of my chords and rhythm. We ended the jam in a great, screeching crescendo. It was wonderful, exhausting, beautiful fun! I forgot for a moment that I was a leadership consultant at a hospital, playing with my CEO, in front of colleagues. Surely, this was where my heart belonged!

"Excellent!" Ravi exclaimed, as we returned to our audience. "Now, let me ask everyone, which of these two sessions did you prefer?"

Pat said, "Duh!"

We all laughed.

"Ravi," I said. "Thanks for this little diversion here. I think it is a great example. If I may, let me share my thoughts on what Ravi's example here means. I think that personality in organizations is just like a musical instrument. In jazz music, every player comes in carrying their own instrument and style—kind of like their own personality—and they're suddenly asked to play along with the rest of the band. Now, if you want sweet, wonderful music, you have to know your instrument, know the key of the song, and you have to practice. If you want discordant music, then you can just show up as we did, and make a lot of noise. Unfortunately, the latter approach is what happens in most organizations. People just show up, plug in, and start playing out of rhythm and harmony. You can't just expect that you can plug in your instrument in an organizational setting and be magically in harmony. People need to practice behavior, just as much as they need to practice musical instruments."

"Exactly," Ravi said. "And what's beautiful about what we're trying to do is that, in LeaderPractice meetings, we want to offer all of us an opportunity to practice and improve in the safety of a supportive group setting, not in a real-time business situation where your job and professional reputation are on the line. That safety is critical, so that you can freely make mistakes and learn from them, just like we did in the first session with all of us banging away in a crazy manner. And, as you could see from the second session, once we become tight, we are in harmony, and that kind of powerful harmony is what builds great teams, as well as great performance and productivity in organizations."

No one responded with words, but heads were bobbing. I think the point had been made.

"Shall we resume our discussion on the ostrich cards?" I asked. "Who wants to go next?"

The Three Gaps between Goals and Greatness

"I will," said Elizabeth. She pulled her ostrich card from her purse and proceeded to tell us what her evaluations had revealed. As we went round the table, it was obvious that people were feeling much more trusting of each other already, exposing themselves and their inner feelings and growing as a group. Although it was an uncomfortable exercise at first, it later became quite fun. The only exception was Janet Knutson, whose scores had exposed her as someone who had an inflated view of her own competency and worth, and who did far more talking than listening. She did not appreciate that. I wish I could have fully understood what was truly going on beneath her uneasy frown. All I can tell you is that she did not seem to be enjoying that process at all.

But I can tell you this, between the jazz, the warm feelings, the trust-building ostrich card discussions, and the excellent pizza that Ravi later ordered, I thought the evening was a whole lot of fun. Bravo for jazz practice!

Pelè Raymond Ugboajah, PhD

The Employees

First thing on Monday morning, Middleville employees were greeted by an all-employees e-mail from Ravi. In that e-mail, he announced that an all-hands meeting was going to take place on Friday to roll out a process called LeaderPractice, which he described as the solution to the ninety-day shut-down warning and challenge that was handed down by the Rural Hospital Commission. He described LeaderPractice as a weekly, mandatory, one-hour team-building exercise that would help us address all of the RHC's concerns and turn the hospital back into an effective organization. Addressing the recent death and emergency situation that set the hospital's problems in motion in the first place, he also announced a policy change that would create a new level of financial compensation and incentive for any doctors and nurses who would be willing to come into the hospital as needed, even if it was not their shift. He also proposed new incentives, rewards, and recognition programs for employees who showcased empathetic and positive team behavior. In conclusion, he thanked the entire organization for the opportunity to serve them and said that he looked forward to meeting them in person on Friday. He ended his e-mail with a famous quote from Peter Drucker:

"According to Peter Drucker, efficiency is about doing things right; while effectiveness is about doing the right things. Within the next ninety days, our vision, mission, and goal here at Middleville Hospital is not just about trying to do lots of things more efficiently. It is about one thing, and one thing only: to become a truly *effective* organization."

As I was reading this in the temporary office I had been assigned, I heard a knock on my door. It was Ruby.

"Hi, stranger!" she said. "You've been gone at work so much, I hardly see you anymore!"

She was right. I had become so engrossed in my leadership consulting work at the hospital that I was spending a lot of time away from home, Ruby, and Junior. The only fortunate part of that situation occurred when Ruby was working, and she and I could plan the occasional quick lunch or coffee break at the hospital cafeteria.

"Well," Ruby said, standing in my doorway. "I hear that you and Ravi are now quite the stars here at the hospital. Everyone loves the new people-oriented programs you guys are rolling out."

"Thanks," I said. I was actually quite happy to get this feedback. "We're doing our best. What exactly are you hearing?"

"Well, the other day, Amy Wells stopped me and mentioned how effective your ostrich cards are turning out to be. She said that whenever she gets really mad at someone on her team and is about to blow her top, she just pulls out her card and smiles."

"That's really good. I'm glad to hear that."

"Speaking of temper," Ruby said. "I've gotta go. We have a really busy day today, and I have a particularly lovable, but cranky patient who needs lots of face time. See you later!"

"Later!" I said, as she shut my door.

The phone rang. It was Amy Wells.

"Have you heard about the incident between Janet Knutson and Pat D'Arcy?"

"No, I haven't," I said.

"May I come to your office and discuss this with you?"

"Certainly, Amy!"

She entered my office within a few minutes and closed the door behind her. I was quickly learning that one of the most prevalent practices in a dysfunctional organization is that doors get closed a lot, and people speak in whispers. I started to wonder if I'd earn a PhD in door shutting before this was all over.

"Well," Amy said. "I want you to know that I really trust you and Ravi, and I really appreciate the work that you two are doing here. I think that you guys are excellent leaders."

"Well, thank you, Amy! That's really nice of you to say. Now what is this about Janet Knutson and Pat D'Arcy?"

"Okay, please don't tell anyone I said this," Amy said, looking at me, waiting for my confirmation of discretion.

"I promise."

"All right. I heard those two shared some very tough words yesterday. Something about Janet being really angry that Pat made her look bad at our last executive team meeting with Ravi. I heard that Janet threatened Pat within an inch of her life and practically left her crying in her office!"

"Wow! Wasn't that the time when Pat joked about Janet being a micromanager during the last meeting?"

"Yes. And here's what you don't know about this organization. Janet might look really thin and frail, but she's very powerful. She has some serious political weight and support among key members of the hospital board, and when she's angry, she can really turn up the heat on people."

"Good for her," I said. "What do you think might happen next?"

"Not sure," Amy said. "But I wouldn't be surprised if something doesn't happen soon with Janet. Don't be deceived by the fact that she is just the H.R. director. For years, Janet has been the real power broker in this organization, and I don't think she is very happy with all this new stuff that you and Ravi are introducing."

"Well, that's interesting!" I said. "I've heard only positive things about our work. I even heard a rumor that people think Ravi and I are doing an okay job."

"In my opinion, you are," Amy said, leaning over and bringing her voice down to a whisper. "But the real question is, do the members of the board think you're doing an okay job?"

Her words gave me pause. I had never considered that anyone —let alone the members of the board—would think it was wrong to include behavior in the mix of things that are measured in an attempt to create a more effective organization. It all seemed so normal to me, and I felt that we were innovating and bringing new, important concepts into practice. At that point, however, I was suddenly reminded of Abigail's words to me on my last day at LeaderPractice. I remembered how she described me as an innovator, and the potential conflicts that could arise in environments where other people might be adapters. She was right. Could Janet's issue simply be that she was an adapter who wasn't comfortable with all the innovation and changes that Ravi and I were rolling out, and the speed with which all of this was occurring?

"Amy, do you think I need to have a one-on-one discussion with Janet Knutson?"

"I really think you do. I don't mean to throw her under the bus, but she's a tough one to talk to or to get along with. I think coming from you, she'll probably listen out of respect for your consulting assignment and in light of the emergency situation the hospital is in right now."

"Thanks for bringing this to my attention, Amy. I'm glad we can trust each other!"

"Anytime," she said, and left my office.

The Three Gaps between Goals and Greatness

I decided to take a quick walk to get to know some of the nurses and staff. I had wanted to make that a scheduled practice but always got behind on work. I pulled out my ostrich card to remind myself that I have a tendency to enjoy working alone. Thank goodness for my ostrich card! I was instantly reminded that even I needed to practice what I was preaching. It was not just a nice to have to walk around and connect socially with people at work. It was a necessity, and because of my particular personality, I realized I had to work extra hard at getting out there and connecting with people.

I stopped at a nurse's station and began to chitchat with Melanie and Samantha, two nurses on duty that day.

"Hey, there, Dr. Ruby's husband!" Melanie joked.

"Yeah, what she said," echoed Samantha.

"Hi, Melanie and Samantha," I said, smiling and reading their names off of their uniforms. "I bet you don't even know my name yet, do you? When will I ever earn my own reputation around here?"

"You got that right, buddy! No, just kidding!" Melanie said. "Of course we know you're Mike. But you're right. I bet a lot of people don't know your name, but they'll never need to. As long as you're Dr. Ruby's husband, you're one of us, and we love ya!"

"Hey, thanks, guys!" I said and walked toward the administrative offices. It occurred to me that I hadn't seen or heard from Ravi all day.

"Hey, Mr. Leadership Consultant." It was Pastor Donahue, sticking his head out of his office.

"Hey, Jake!"

"I heard that people are really excited that you and Ravi are here! Great job!"

"Thanks, Jake. I just hope we can turn all this good will into positive results before our time runs out. How's the purchasing department doing?"

"We're great," he said. "Which reminds me—which Sunday morning are you and Ruby going to come and visit our church? I'd love to see you there!"

"I think we'll take you up on that, Jake. Maybe next week."

"Great!"

"Hey, Jake, Have you seen Ravi today?"

"No," Jake said. "I heard that he's out sick today."

I walked past the administrative offices, knowing that Ravi wouldn't be in. It then occurred to me that if he was out sick, then he probably sent this morning's all-employee e-mail announcement from home. I greeted and joked with different members of staff along the way back to my office. I even stopped to say hello to Angela, one of the oldest people in the hospital. From what I had heard, she was in her late nineties and was a member of the retirement team, a group of retired people who volunteered at the hospital and did anything and everything that needed an extra hand. I always admired how people could reach a place in their lives when they were willing to do things purely for others, without even the slightest hint of a selfish motive.

"Hello, Mike," said Angela, her wrinkled face beaming with joy. I was surprised she even knew my name.

"Hi there, Angela. I hope you're having a great day!" I said.

"Yes, I am," she said, "and even more so because you and your lovely Dr. Ruby are here. All the employees think that you are doing a fantastic job!"

"Thank you," I said, and I meant that from the bottom of my heart. I watched her walk slowly but surely back to her station and sit down, with purpose, poise, and an unbending determination to give the last few years of her life to the worthy cause of helping others. I thought briefly about Ravi's words of wisdom, about his new path of focusing on helping others, one life at a time. This, I thought, must be the same path that Angela was on. My eyes grew quickly and surprisingly misty, and I quickly walked back toward my office, wiping my eyes innocently as though some lint had found its way into them. No one needed to know how moved I was by Angela and her kind words. I was not about to let Middleville employees see their leadership consultant in tears.

Pelè Raymond Ugboajah, PhD

The Behavior Gap

"We have just three days left!" Ravi said. He had called a brief catch-up meeting with the leadership team on Tuesday morning since he had been out of the office sick on Monday. "Before we roll this out to all employees next Monday, I want all members of the executive and middle management teams to know exactly what our plan is. Mike, what's your plan?"

"I've sent out a recurring schedule for an all-managers meeting at noon Tuesday, Wednesday, and Friday. If all goes well, on Friday, we'll have our first LeaderPractice meeting."

"Janet," Ravi said. "Will that work for you?"

"If that's what you want, we'll do it," she said, wearing a poker face.

"Anyone with a conflict?"

Everyone shook their heads.

"All right then. Let's meet today at noon and wrap this thing up!"

"How are you feeling, Ravi?" I asked, as we began to file out of his office, "What happened yesterday?"

"Oh, I had some weird chest pain in the morning, probably some acid reflux or something." he said. "I could have probably come in toward the end of the day, but I wanted to conserve all my energy for the next few days. We really have to knock this thing out of the park by Friday or else this plan won't get executed. Let's get it done, Mike!"

"Aye, aye, boss!"

The managers meeting started promptly at noon in the grand meeting room. All the members of the executive team were in attendance—Jake Donahue, Amy Wells, Elizabeth Pierce, Pat D'Arcy, and Janet Knutson. Also in attendance were seven department managers. This was to be the first rollout session for the LeaderPractice solution to the entire leadership group at Middleville Hospital.

"Good afternoon," I said, scanning the faces in front of me. The meeting room was hot and stuffy, but we opened up a window to let some air in. Ravi sat at the back, behind everyone. I guessed he did that so that he could have the best possible view of how our message was being received.

"Let's start with the obvious," I said. "Middleville Hospital is a small rural organization with excellent, well-trained, and qualified physicians, staff, and administrative personnel. On the surface, we have lots of money in the bank, solid infrastructure and technology, and the capability to achieve healthcare excellence in this community. Yet, something is amiss. We seem to have a gap between what we say we want to achieve and what we actually achieve. We have low employee morale, low performance reports, and worst of all, the RHC has now given us less than ninety days to clean up our act or be shut down. To be extremely blunt, we have found that dysfunction here at Middleville is the norm, not the exception. Does everyone agree with that picture?"

I could see people nodding their heads. Not one to let a great interactive opportunity pass, I raised my hand, and reiterated my question.

The Three Gaps between Goals and Greatness

"With a show of hands, how many people here believe that the picture I just painted is 100% accurate?"

All hands went up, albeit some more slowly than others. Ravi's hand shot high up in the air, more quickly and confidently than everyone else's. He wore his rueful grin with sarcasm.

"All right. Now, who can tell us what is causing the problem here? Not you, Ravi!"

There was a collective chuckle in the room.

"I think our employees are complacent," said one of the department managers. "They think that just because there is a shortage of people in our small town that they will have their jobs forever, regardless of their performance."

"Interesting. Anyone else?"

"I disagree," said Pat D'Arcy, looking at Janet Knutson with an evil eye. "I think our employees are taking their cues from management. We are the ones setting the tone. If they are complacent, then it is because we are."

"Excellent!" I said. "Pat, you ought to come teach this stuff! That is precisely the point! The reason we are meeting first as an extended management team is that, frankly, if we can't fix these issues at our level, we can't expect anything to change within the organization. Only with great leadership is our success possible."

I walked over the chalkboard and wrote in bold letters:

THE BEHAVIOR GAP

"Who can tell us in one sentence what this means?" I asked.

Elizabeth Pierce raised her hand. "The behavior gap is the first of the three gaps that stand between our organization's goals and our ability to achieved them."

"Precisely!" I said. "And what are those three gaps?"

"Behavior, habits, and community!" Pastor Donahue said.

"That's right, and today, we are going to focus on the behavior gap. Tomorrow, we'll talk about the habits gap, and on Thursday, we'll wrap up with the community gap. As we all know, greatness is only possible for us as an organization if our goals are achieved, and the number one thing stopping us from achieving our goals is not even visible to us. We can see and measure our performance, such as how frequently nurses and doctors round on patients. But how do we measure behavior—the one thing that gets in the way of good teamwork and interpersonal relationships? And to make matters worse, we all ignore behavior, allowing it to fester in the background and cause all kinds of trouble for us. So, if we are going to ever achieve greatness, we're going to have to bridge the three gaps between goals and greatness, starting with the behavior gap." I walked back to the chalkboard and wrote out the full problem.

> The behavior gap occurs when organizations do not make the time to measure, track, and develop behaviors that will positively affect performance.

"All right," I said, with my marker at the ready to capture more ideas. "So now we know the problem. What is the solution? Amy, any thoughts?"

"Actually, I was going to say, that the first thing we should do is become aware of what our behaviors and personalities actually are."

"Precisely," I said and turned to the department managers. "I know that some of you are hearing this for the first time, but I'd like to know how you think we might come to learn our personalities and behavior patterns?"

"Myers Briggs!"

"DISC!"

The Three Gaps between Goals and Greatness

"Actually, those are a great start," I said. "But what we want is to capture even deeper nuances than those tests reveal. We want to know what positive and negative aspects of our behavior are at play at all times. Most importantly, we want to know which of our dominant traits might either help or destroy our leadership efforts, especially when we are under stress. So, you're on the right track! We need to get detailed, psychometric leadership evaluations done on selected members in our leadership teams. We also need to perform 360-degree surveys to find out not only what the psych instruments say, but also what our own peers, managers, and subordinates think of us. Without that kind of information, we just won't ever know how we are perceived in reality." I went over to my pile of documents and pulled out some photocopies I'd made.

"I'm going to be passing out a table with the three gaps over the next three days, so we can discuss them all in one printed format. The document contained a description of the problem and the solution around the first gap: the behavior gap.

The Three Gaps	Description	Solution
BEHAVIOR	The Behavior Gap occurs when organizations do not make the time to measure, track, and develop leadership behaviors that will positively affect performance.	1. Assessment - Pick leaders and teams, and perform psychometric/360 personality assessments. 2. Pick the top 3 leadership behaviors and the top 3 individual personality behaviors that will support good interpersonal interactions and the goals of the organization. 3. Assign measurement criteria and align all 'intangible' behaviors with all the 'tangible' performance goals of the organization. 4. Carry an 'Ostrich Card' to keep these top 6 behaviors top of mind at all times.

After I passed out the documents, I walked among the group and began to explain what was in them.

"The behavior gap didn't start here," I said. "It started way back when we were kids. We were all taught performance-focused things like math and reading and science, but no one sat us down and talked about personality and behavior. Somehow, we were all supposed to just figure that out when we got into the workplace after years of just winging it and developing what might actually be bad behavior habits along the way! Our goal now is to unlearn unproductive behaviors and practice those behaviors that we agree will increase our effectiveness and productivity as a team. Okay, here's your first quiz for the day. Who can tell me what an ostrich card is?"

Elizabeth Pierce jumped into the conversation. "An ostrich card is a small, business-card-sized summary of your top three leadership and top three individual behaviors."

"Precisely!" We need to carry the ostrich card around to remind us that our inherent behaviors are working all the time to either support or derail our leadership efforts. If we can see at all times who we are, and who we want to be, then we won't end up like the ostrich, which foolishly hides its head in the sand and somehow thinks that its body is also hidden. Unfortunately, its body is still exposed to the lion that comes by and gobbles it up. Who can tell me, in this parable, what the body and the lion represent?"

"The behavior gap," someone said.

"Excellent. And what does the sand represent?"

"Being busy in our daily work."

"Exactly. We have to constantly be aware that our work is not an excuse for remaining blind to the ongoing behaviors that can derail our work in the first place."

I could see people taking notes and nodding. Our message was sinking in. I walked back to the chalkboard and began a table of behaviors.

The Three Gaps between Goals and Greatness

"Here," I said, "is a list of twenty well-known behaviors that can either build or destroy good leadership, and therefore, the best-intentioned organizational plans. Each of us will probably have one, two or three of these on our ostrich cards. Notice that in the third, blank column, there is a space for suggestions on how to avoid responding with destructive behaviors when opportunities arise. This is most useful when you're under stress. Instead of reacting from your destructive behavior comfort zone, you can just consult your ostrich card, where you can find easy instructions on how to avoid a negative or explosive situation.

BUILDING BEHAVIOR	DESTRUCTIVE BEHAVIOR
Empathetic	Self-Important
Optimistic	Pessimistic
Forthcoming	Uncommunicative
Delegating	Micromanaging
Dependable	Unpredictable
Courageous	Overly-Nice
Respectful	Sycophant
Amicable	Combative
Trusting	Detached
Truthfulness	Ambiguous

"Now, let's do an exercise," I said. "I call this the commitment exercise. Each of us will take a piece of paper and write down a personal commitment to spend the rest of the day watching our behavior. Ask yourself, which of these building or destructive behaviors do you sometimes or habitually display? At the end of the day, I want you to write down your observations from your own behavior and bring that in for tomorrow's conversation on the habits gap. Do I have your commitment to do that?"

No one said anything. I strolled toward the group, looking everyone squarely in the eyes. I wasn't going to let this entire discussion pass from one ear to the next and out of their heads the way most training sessions go. I wanted this stuff to stick, no matter how uncomfortable it might seem to them at the moment.

"Raise your hand if you are 100% committed to tracking your behavior for the rest of the day, identifying which of these behaviors might apply to you, and reporting back to us first thing tomorrow morning."

Finally, everyone raised their hands.

"Great. Tomorrow, we will expect to see everyone's behavior reports. Ravi, I think we're done."

"Excellent, Mike. Thank you," Ravi said. "Any questions?"

There were none. One down, two to go!

The Habits Gap

irst thing Wednesday morning, all department heads and executive team members were in the meeting room. After the great start we had the day before, I was very hopeful that this would be another solid session. Ravi closed the room door once everyone was seated. He then motioned for me to proceed with the day's discussion.

"Good morning, everyone!" I announced. They rumbled in response.

"All right. Who remembered to monitor and record their behavior yesterday?"

Only one hand was raised. It was Pastor Donahue.

"Do we have only one person here who kept their commitment?"

No response. Lots of eyes avoided my gaze.

"Well, this proves a very important point, doesn't it? Who can tell us what point this proves?"

Elizabeth responded. "Well, it looks like this program isn't that popular after all!"

"You're right about the popularity issue," said Ravi. "And therein lies the point. Obviously, monitoring our behavior is not something we're used to doing, or we wouldn't need to learn about it in the first place. We need to break old habits and learn new ones if we are to succeed."

"That's right," I said. "I'm not in the least surprised that most of you did not keep your public, written commitment to us from yesterday. To be perfectly honest, this kind of laissez-faire accountability is typical in dysfunctional organizations, and we've all admitted that we are currently dysfunctional, so I'm not saying anything new. However, we have to hold each other collectively accountable if we're ever going to make the transition from goals to greatness."

Ravi joined in. "Please let this be a reminder that the ostrich is still exposed, even though it buries its head in the sand. I'd like to see this assignment repeated after today's lesson. Please have this assignment ready for our discussion of the third gap tomorrow." Ravi turned toward me. "All right, Mike. Carry on."

"Okay," I said. "Let's get straight to work." I uncovered the diagrams and tables we drew the day before. "As we agreed yesterday, our organization has talented, knowledgeable, hardworking people, and yet somehow our performance is lagging behind the competition. To make matters worse, we have less than seventy days to improve the performance appraisal handed down from the RHC. Anyone feel the urgency here?"

Another rumble. Heads were nodding.

"Great. Yesterday, we covered the behavior gap. We all agreed that behavior is the unseen power that is ever present and can either be used for good, or if allowed to fester unaddressed, can destroy our entire company. We therefore agreed that we need to first become aware of it and use certain tools to make it an integral part of the things that we measure, track, and develop in our organization, right?"

"Right!"

"All right," I said. "Today, we're going to do something a little different." I opened the IT locker in the corner of the room and pulled out an eighty-eight-key Yamaha piano keyboard I had kept there. A murmur grew and rolled around the room. Pastor Donahue couldn't help himself. "Great! He's gonna give us a jazz concert!"

"Actually, I'm not," I said. "You are!"

I asked for a volunteer, someone who had zero piano-playing skills whatsoever. Amy, always the fun-loving one, raised her hand and I called her forward. Ravi had an interesting, expectant look on his face. He was no doubt enjoying the fact that I had picked up on his musical instrument parable and was about to apply the analogy again.

"Amy," I asked. "Have you ever played piano in your life?"

"Nope!"

"Perfect. Please play the alphabet song for us, starting from this key here." I pointed to middle C for her on the piano keyboard and started snapping my fingers to a steady beat. "Also, play it at this tempo."

She began slowly picking at the notes with her index finger, at first ignoring my tempo altogether. She struggled until she found some of the right notes, and then struggled some more until she began to discover the relationships between the notes. Once she found some of the right notes, she started struggling to match my tempo, and was thrown completely off by the two simultaneous tasks of finding the right notes and playing at a certain speed. A few minutes later, she gave up and laughed.

"I can't do this to save my life!" she said.

"Yes, you can," I said. Watch my hands. I placed my entire right hand over the keyboard with my thumb on middle C. Without moving my hand at all, I placed my pinky on the G note and played the entire pattern, using all of my fingers for the appropriate notes.

I then played it faster and faster, until I was playing extremely fast. I then stopped suddenly as quickly as I had started.

"Now, let me show you how to do that." I placed her fingers down on the keyboard in the right configuration and started showing her how to play the pattern without fumbling and moving her entire hand all over the keyboard. I showed her how to rely on the different individual fingers of her hand to play individual notes. I also showed her how to first start by slowing everything down, and then working up in speed gradually. Once she adopted the new process, she started playing it a bit better.

"Now, repeat that as many times as you can," I said.

She began repeating that first phrase, and pretty soon, she was playing faster and faster until she was surprised to find that she was almost as fast as I had been. She stopped suddenly, and everyone clapped for her. I thanked her for the demonstration and asked her to take her seat.

"What was the moral of that little demonstration, folks?"

"Having talent makes a difference!" someone said, and we all laughed.

"How about practice makes perfect?" someone else said.

"Precisely!" I said. This is not rocket science. What Amy just learned is a basic building block to how she or anyone here could become the next Bach or Handel or Prince or Stevie Wonder! But there is something that lies between what she did today and her ability to reach the legendary greatness of a Beethoven. Who can tell me what that is?"

"A couple hundred years of practice?" Pat said, and we laughed again.

"Focused repetition?" Ravi said.

The Three Gaps between Goals and Greatness

"Absolutely!" I said, and walked over to the board to write the following:

> The habits gap occurs when organizations don't create time for leaders to repetitively practice desired behaviors until they become positive habits.

"If Amy sits here for hours and spends several days practicing this simple scale based on having been taught the right way to do it, eventually, she will be able to do it without thinking. That's how our brains work. It'll become second nature to her, just like what happens when you learn to ride a bicycle. Who can tell us what is actually happening in the brain during this learning process?"

No one responded.

"All right. Well, this happens to be one of my favorite topics, but I'll keep it short and simple. I call it *mind transfer*. Amy's *conscious* mind would be transferring the piano playing skill I just taught her to her *unconscious* mind. The unconscious mind is what takes over once you no longer have to consciously think about riding a bicycle. Think about when you speak; notice how you don't actually have to think about how your mouth is forming the words you're going to use to make a point. That's because your unconscious mind is doing all of those mechanical tasks for you. If this were a new language, your conscious mind, which is actually the less powerful of the two minds, would struggle to make it work. The same happens with behavior. The brain needs to repeat things to hold them in short-term memory. If we repeat the right behaviors and practice the right responses to certain situations, we eventually build *muscle memory* in our behavior patterns, just like what happens in our fingers on the piano keyboard. The ultimate goal is to use repetition to turn appropriate, successful behaviors into habits while learning new habits to help us mitigate our own inherent, destructive behaviors and responses. Everyone get that?"

I had some heads nodding back at me. I went up to my pile of documents and handed out another sheet of paper that contained the six steps for piano and behavior practice:

"The basic rules for practicing behavior until perfection are no different than practicing the piano. There are essentially six steps in the practice process for changing or growing specific behavior goals. Here is a chart that compares the habit-forming process on a piano to the same process when it comes to working on behavior:"

Step	Piano Practice	Behavior Practice
1.	Learn a new piano phrase	Learn a new leadership behavior, model, or skill
2.	Divide the phrase into left and right hand parts	Divide the new skill into its constituent model parts
3.	Reduce tempo	Reduce risk through role-play with fewer, trusted partners
4.	Repeat until new habits form	Repeat until new habits form
5.	Assemble left and right hands and repeat until combined habits form	Assemble model parts and repeat until habits form
6.	Perform at the right tempo, and in real situations	Perform in the workplace, in real situations

"Any questions?" There were none. I passed out the next sheet, which contained the previous day's information on the behavior gap, as well today's information on the habits gap.

The Three Gaps	Description	Solution
HABITS	The Habits Gap occurs when organizations don't encourage leaders to practice behavior until they become positive habits.	1. Start with a 'Clean Slate' by announcing goals, seeking forgiveness from teammates, and asking for help. 2. Write down your personal change commitment statement including behavior goals and measurability. 3. Break desired behavior changes down into smaller solution steps. 4. Repeat the behavior change steps and measure and document progress daily during the workweek.

"All right," I said. "Let's define the habits gap. Remember that our goal is to identify these gaps and discuss strategies for closing them, which will open the way for us to become an effective organization. As you can see from your handout, the habits gap occurs when organizations don't encourage leaders to practice behavior until positive habits become ingrained. So, invariably, what happens is that no matter what we learn in seminars, we usually return to our comfort-zone behaviors, which could hurt our performance. Also, practicing on the job is not a safe way to develop habits because you don't have the luxury of experimentation and making mistakes. The big problem is that if we don't replace bad habits with good habits, nothing will change in the organization. Any questions on the habit gap?"

Pat D'Arcy raised her hand. "Can you give me an example of how the habits gap shows itself? I'm a bit confused about this one."

"Great question, Pat!" I walked over and wrote the following on the chalkboard:

> You can't learn to play soccer at a seminar!

"How many of you have made New Year's resolutions, but within a few days or weeks, you had completely abandoned them?"

Heads were nodding.

"What do you think happened?"

"You return to old habits," Pat said.

"Exactly. You can't learn to play soccer at a seminar! It's far too easy for us to agree on what we want to change in a training environment or on New Year's Eve, but unless we put the new behaviors needed to accomplish those goals into consistent practice, nothing will happen."

"Thanks, Mike!" said Pat. "Makes sense to me!"

"Okay," I said. "You can see from the document in front of you that there are four steps to solving the habits problem. First you have to create a clean-slate environment by publicly announcing your goals to a trusted cohort group, seeking forgiveness for difficult interactions with others, and frankly, asking for people around you to commit to helping you monitor your changes along the way. Next, you need to actually write down a personal change commitment statement and have that ready for our LeaderPractice meetings. Over time, we'll follow the LeaderPractice manual for various leadership topics and behaviors, and break them down into small, measurable pieces. Finally, we will repeat these solutions over and over in a safe, supportive environment until we get them right. Now, who can tell me how and in what forum we will be repeating these behaviors?"

Elizabeth raised her hand. "In the weekly meetings?"

"Exactly! And we'll cover that tomorrow when we talk about the community gap. Any questions?"

No one had any. We were doing well. The mood in the room was charged, positive, and ripe for action. Two down, one to go!

Pelè Raymond Ugboajah, PhD

The Community Gap

"Has anyone seen Janet Knutson?" I asked. It was 9:00 A.M. on Thursday, and we were just about to get started on the third and final day of our crash leadership course on the three gaps between goals and greatness. Everyone was in the room, except Janet Knutson.

"I saw her this morning," Elizabeth said. "She said she wouldn't be attending the meeting today."

"Ravi, did you know she was going to be absent today?"

"No," he said, with a surprised look on his face. "I certainly did not. We need our director of human resources here to fully understand this information. I'll go talk with her and get to the bottom of this. Proceed with your training," Ravi got up to leave.

"Thanks, Ravi," I said, as he left. "All right. Who's ever been a member of Toastmasters?" I asked. Pastor Donahue was the only one who raised his hand.

"Jake, can you tell us a bit about your experience at Toastmasters?"

"As a pastor," Jake Donahue said, "Toastmasters was pretty much a godsend for me. I really needed to get over my fear of public speaking and a friend recommended I join. When I got over my inhibitions about speaking in front of a group and finally got started, I was surprised at how much I actually enjoyed it. It was great fun watching myself and others struggle at first, and then grow slowly but surely into much better speaking ability over time. I think that my speaking skills improved 150% as a result of practicing in front of others and getting feedback from them."

"Thanks, Jake," I said, and turned to address the rest of the group. "You'll find that there are tons of people the world over who will tell you the same thing. Both Ravi and I have certainly experienced the difference it makes to learn public speaking within a Toastmasters community of people. The value of community learning is self-evident and intuitive, and as such, I've always wondered why organizations don't create opportunities for people to practice and improve behavioral skills in community settings. It seems that people don't seem to want to jump on a bandwagon until it's already gone, so we are going to have to prove the viability of community as a leadership development tool by adopting it here first."

"How do you propose we do that?" Elizabeth said.

"By forming regular practice teams. Only, instead of working on work, we will work on ourselves."

"And how would you stop that from turning into a circus?" she asked.

"Well, first of all, these meetings start at strategic leadership levels. Second, they will be following a clearly written leadership manual that walks them through specific group exercises. There will be a lot of structure to these meetings, and they will always be measurable in terms of how much positive impact is being achieved by the organization. Let's start by defining what we mean by the community gap." I strolled to the chalkboard and wrote:

It takes a village to raise a child. —African Proverb

"Who can tell us what this means?" I asked.

"Hillary Clinton will be the next president?" someone said. We shared a group chuckle.

"This African proverb basically describes the concept of community as one of the most powerful enablers we know of for learning and development. Community provides the safety and low-risk, supportive environment we all need to practice and improve our organizational behaviors. I'll be honest with you; I have struggled my entire professional life to understand why organizations would set performance development goals, and then allow a Darwinian free market for behavioral development on the job. New discoveries in brain science tell us clearly that people don't develop well or learn much under stress. Basically, as a species, we don't multitask very well, which is why it is so dangerous to text and drive. If we don't provide specific times for working on behavior, how can we expect people to appropriately develop the right team environments, especially while results and organizational effectiveness are on the line?"

I walked back to the chalkboard and wrote the following definition.

> The community gap occurs when organizations don't create communities of practice where positive behaviors can be safely developed.

I passed out the handout for the day.

The Three Gaps	Description	Solution
COMMUNITY	The Community Gap occurs when organizations don't create communities of practice where positive behaviors can be safely developed.	1. Regular structured LeaderPractice Meetings (Weekly recommended). 2. Impromptu Leadership Simulations, Games, and Role-play. 3. Prepared Leadership Teachable Moment Speeches. 4. Instant group feedback, mentoring, evaluations, encouragement, and accountability.

"This is where everything really comes together," I said. "The community that we are talking about here is essentially what happens in a LeaderPractice meeting. These will be regular, hourly, low-risk meetings where selected members of our leadership group will get together to follow a structured process of leadership learning, simulations, and feedback. You can see the basic structure for a LeaderPractice meeting in the solutions section of the community gap. First, we will have impromptu simulations, games, and role-play. Next, we will have one leader present a prepared teachable-moment speech describing an example of positive leadership behaviors he or she observed. Finally, we conclude by providing instant group feedback and evaluations to the participants. Any questions so far?"

No one had any questions.

The Three Gaps between Goals and Greatness

"Any observations?" I asked.

"Yes," said one of the department managers. It was Sally, the IT manager. "How could we integrate technology into this? For example, you have Facebook, and Linkedin and other social networking sites that are defining what we mean by community in today's world. How could this LeaderPractice community leverage those kinds of trends?"

"Excellent point!" I said. "You took the next section, right out of my mouth!"

"Uff dah!" she joked. "My mistake. Please go ahead."

"As Sally very correctly noticed, the weekly meetings are only 50% of the LeaderPractice solution. In today's world, the other half of what we'll do is Internet and software based. We will have software that will track all of the things we've talked about over the past three days. We will track our inherent behavioral assessments, our performance and behavioral goals, our ostrich profiles, our progress on habit development, and the accountability and results of our LeaderPractice community exercises. All of this will be done in a secure online environment to support our weekly in-person interactions. Sally is absolutely right. Software technology is at the heart of how we intend to close the community gap."

I could see heads nodding. People were connecting with this stuff. "Has anyone here ever used software to manage goal setting and development?" A few hands were raised. "Well, the kind of software we're talking about is in that same family. You create goals, cascading and aligning them all the way down from the CEO to the average employee. Tracking and measuring goals is a well-known, successful way to get things done in organizations, but the software and processes out there unfortunately are missing three elements. There are three gaps that are not being managed today in organizations, which invariably leave them to be less than effective.

With one voice, I'd like everyone to tell us what those three gaps are."

"Behavior, habits, and community!" the group replied in unison.

"Exactly!" I said, with my arms outstretched, as though we had just scored a goal in a soccer game. "I think we're ready to go! Tomorrow is our first LeaderPractice meeting, and Monday will be our first announcement to the organization about our new concept of focusing on behavior as much as performance. Thanks for participating in this introductory training."

People clapped. It was great to see the look of appreciation on a few of their faces. Something new was certainly afoot at Middleville. The only issue was whether or not we could put these things into practice and achieve results in less than two months. The clock was now officially ticking. The race was on!

I stopped over at Ravi's office right after the training session to find out what he might have learned about Janet Knutson's absence.

"So, what happened?" I asked.

"Absolutely unbelievable!" Ravi said, visibly disturbed. "You would never believe what she told me!"

"What did she say?"

"She said that she had better things to do!"

"What?" I exclaimed.

"Yes! She told me to my face that these mandatory meetings I called were not worth her time."

"What are you going to do about this, Ravi? Janet's behavior is bringing down the team's morale."

"I've told her in no uncertain terms that I will not tolerate insubordination. The first rule of leadership is that what you permit, you promote. I will not permit this. Rest assured, she is not going to get away with this kind of behavior. One more slip like this, and she's fired. I've put her on notice."

The Three Gaps between Goals and Greatness

I shook my head. Janet Knutson had seemed to be a problem right from the beginning. From her behavior, I surmised that she was not happy that Ravi and I were here and charged with the task of straightening out the hospital's issues. It almost seemed as though she were envious of something or that she felt she ought to be more centrally involved in the leadership and decisions around what we were doing. I couldn't quite figure her out.

"Ravi, may I go and talk with her?"

"Sure. But nothing changes. If she won't even attend a LeaderPractice meeting, how can we help her be successful in this organization? Frankly, if I see one more negative, team-busting behavior out of Janet Knutson, we will need to find a new director of human resources!"

Pelè Raymond Ugboajah, PhD

She's a Good Nurse, But…

"You have to get the right people on the bus!" said Janet Knutson, her face twisted in a snarl. I was sitting in her office, first thing on Friday morning, listening to her sermon about how to build the right organizational culture at Middleville Hospital. I had visited Janet to find out why she had not been attending our meetings lately, and to invite her to the first weekly LeaderPractice meeting for the executive team that was scheduled for the afternoon. I explained to her that as the director of human resources, her support and participation would be critical in helping us get the organization and its employees back on line for success.

"When employees are out of line," she said, with a look of what seemed like pleasure on her face, "you simply have to fire them. I won't permit low performance. This leadership development thing is for the birds. People are born the way they are. The best solution is just to fire them—it's worked every time!"

"Isn't that a little drastic?" I asked. "How about working with people to mitigate destructive behaviors and encourage positive ones?"

"Who has time for that?" Her voice was getting louder with every sentence. "I'm way too busy with union issues and other tangible workforce concerns. I have no time to keep worrying about these pesky behavioral problems! People need to just grow up and get things done. It's about performance, not behavior! We're measured by performance around here, Mike, not behavior!"

I kept quiet for a moment, eager to have Janet return to a lower, less volatile tone. Her words reverberated in my brain. *It's about performance, not behavior.* I think right there and then, her words encapsulated the gulf between us. It reminded me so much of what Ravi had said about the people at LeaderTraits: that leaders in our world pretty much fell into two categories—lizards who cared more about performance and bush rats who actually cared about people. Janet's words also reminded me of the ostrich and the lion. It was clear to me now exactly which side of the world Janet Knutson was from. Janet Knutson was a lizard. She was also an ostrich with her head in the sand of performance, willfully ignoring the importance and presence of people issues.

"Janet," I said, picking my words carefully. I was still taken by surprise at the sheer volume and intensity this skinny woman packed into her voice. And what a temper! I didn't want to ever have to cross Janet Knutson. However, I had a job to do, and I was determined to get to the bottom of why she was disobeying our new interim CEO.

"Remember when we first met," I said, "and you explained to me the concept of the "good" nurse with behavior struggles?"

"Yes," she said.

"In a perfect world, would you agree that the place where good performance meets good behavior would be our sweet spot?"

"I guess so."

"Take a look at this," I said, as I pulled out a presentation slide I had been working on:

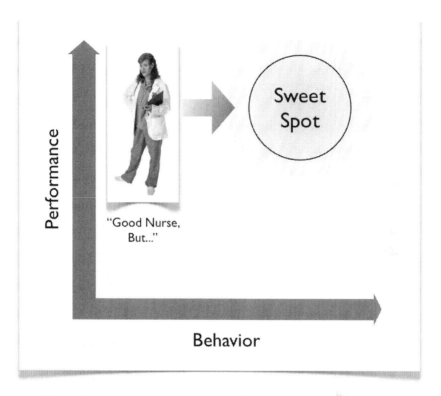

"This diagram represents an employee's performance on the *y-axis*, and their behavior on the *x-axis*. Your "good nurse" example would be high on performance and low on behavior, right?"

"Right."

"Okay. The sweet spot to the right of her is where we need everyone to be, starting with this leadership team. Don't you think there is value in improving behavior so that your "good" nurse can truly be "good" all around?"

"I guess so," she said, nodding her head.

"In that case, we agree on the basics. Now, remember you promised me that you were going to try to work on your own behavior issues—your temper and your micromanaging style?"

She nodded.

"How has that been going for you?"

"Honestly, not very well," she said. "At first, I tried to stay out of people's details, but darn it, some of our people need to really just do their jobs!"

She was livid. Apparently, since we met, certain people in the organization had not been doing their jobs, and it frustrated her to no end. I noticed that she was actually more frustrated now and much nastier than she was when I first met her. I supposed that by trying to change her own behavior, she was performing outside of her comfort zone, and this was providing her with a lot more frustration than when she had simply been a card-carrying, angry micromanager.

"Maybe you should return to being an angry micromanager," I told her, a bit sarcastically. "You are obviously not enjoying the process of trying to change your behavior on your own." I don't think she took that well, and I could tell my welcome was slowly wearing out. But I pressed on. "What you really need is lasting behavior change, not temporary change. Would you agree?"

I could see her thoughtfully nodding her head. I then asked her to tell me what she thought she could do to bring about a more lasting change. After a few moments of uncomfortable silence, I asked her another question.

"What does it take to go from not knowing how to ride a bicycle to mastering it?"

She shook her head.

"Repetition?"

"Exactly! Now, how about playing the piano?"

"Practice?"

"Exactly! Now, how about public speaking, for example, at a Toastmasters club?"

"Feedback from peers?"

"Precisely! So you get the concept of needing to repeat physical skills to form habits and the advantage of doing so within a supportive, safe community of people. Now, how about perfecting a behavioral, leadership skill, like reducing micromanagement?"

Her eyes lit up. I could see the light bulb go off in her head. I felt as though I had finally connected with her heart, not just her mind.

"You mean you think I should practice this behavioral skill and repeat it over and over, just like learning to ride a bike?"

I nodded, looking her squarely in the eyes. Exactly," I said. "So far, you've been winging it, leading by instinct and gut feel. You haven't spent the time to develop specific leadership habits that might improve your leadership performance. All skills, whether physical or behavioral, are made permanent only when they become habits in our minds. In music and sports, we call that transfer of skills into habits *muscle-memory*, which is when your fingers or legs seem to have a mind of their own. What's really happening behind the scenes is that your mind has transferred the skill you've just learned from your conscious mind to your unconscious mind, which is where the "autopilot" magic occurs, and which is why a person is able to play the piano or ride a bike, or slam-dunk a basketball without consciously thinking about it."

Her eyes were starting to gloss over.

"What you need," I told her, "is leadership practice. Are you willing to join us in a safe, supportive LeaderPractice community of practice this afternoon?"

She looked around suspiciously at her desk for a few minutes, and responded in the quietest voice I'd ever heard her use so far.

"No, Mike," she said, in what almost seemed like a sad tone.

"The CEO will not be happy about this, Janet."

"That's his problem!" she snarled back at me, suddenly coming back to life.

I could see that our conversation was at an end. I thanked her for her time and quietly left the room.

Our first LeaderPractice meeting started at 1:00 P.M. sharp. Everyone was there: Ravi, Pastor Donahue, Elizabeth Pierce, Amy Wells, and Pat D'Arcy. Everyone, that is, except Janet Knutson. Ravi betrayed no emotion about Janet's absence, and simply asked me to go ahead and start the meeting.

"Hello, everyone!" I said, mustering all the positive enthusiasm I could after my meeting with Janet. "There will be four sections to our meeting today. During the first section we will give each other brief introductory updates from our ostrich cards. The second section is where we will do some impromptu, simulated role-playing. This will give one or two of us a chance to practice responses to stressful or surprising work situations. When we're done with this section, everyone will record his or her observations, so we can give the actors feedback at the end of the meeting. The next section will involve us picking a leadership topic, and each person will give a quick, two-minute account on how he or she would handle that particular situation. The final section of the meeting will be an opportunity for a prepared report called a teachable leadership moment. The report presenter will share with us a specific leadership incident in which their behavior was tested, and how he or she handled that situation. All of the evaluations, simulations, role-plays, and behavioral advice and suggestions will be taken out of this LeaderPractice manual I've prepared. At the end of the meeting, we'll evaluate the meeting and give each other feedback and suggestions. Finally, we'll vote and present a leader of the day award to the person with the best evaluation from the rest of us. Any questions?"

There were no questions, so we got started. Our meeting was fun, engaging, and surprising proof to both Ravi and I regarding the pure magic that occurs when people get together and work on

The Three Gaps between Goals and Greatness

growing personally and professionally in a safe, nonjudgmental, supportive community of practice. Ravi and I glanced at each other at the end of the meeting with a look that said *yes!* Even without Janet Knutson, our first LeaderPractice meeting was a wild success.

Pelè Raymond Ugboajah, PhD

Results

The next Monday's all-hands meeting was very effective for setting the right organizational tone and vision within the workforce. All Middleville employees were briefed on new organizational expectations for accountability, performance, and effectiveness. Ravi explained the basics of the LeaderPractice process that would be started at the leadership level, and encouraged everyone to adopt the same vision of focusing on behavior as much as performance. In the end, he articulated a clear goal of not only improving the RHC scores but also setting the organization on a course to become a recognized healthcare leader in the region. Employees were motivated, hopeful, and positive about the future. There was only one downside to the meeting— Janet Knutson, the director of human resources, was conspicuously absent.

Over the next few weeks, things began to turn around at Middleville Hospital. We installed a new enterprise software package that would manage organizational goals, aligned, and cascaded all the way from the CEO's goals down to individual employee tasks. We configured the new software package to include the management and measurement of behavior alongside performance goals, and we held weekly LeaderPractice meetings to practice our process of closing the behavior, habits, and community gaps. Business execution began to proceed flawlessly!

Patient health indicators were improving, and patients themselves began to report more positively about how they were treated in exit interviews. Nurses and doctors started improving team interactions, including standing in for colleagues on shifts that weren't theirs—correcting the problem that created the urgency in the first place. Morale was improving, and hope was beginning to replace the fear and despair that had been the norm at Middleville Hospital. The best news came on a Monday morning when I was having a conversation with Ravi in his office. Ravi was right in the middle of making a statement when the phone rang.

"Hello, this is Ravi," he said. Someone said something on the other end of the line.

"What?" Ravi asked, brimming with excitement. "Excellent! Thank you very much. Please send the reports over immediately!"

I asked Ravi what he was so excited about.

"Congratulations, my dear Dr. Mike Jordan," he said. "The Rural Hospital Commission has just lifted our moratorium on happiness! We have been cleared. The ninety day sink-or-swim period has been lifted!"

"You mean the hospital is saved?"

"Technically, yes. Although, they are still watching, so we can't backslide. The fact is, based on patient exit reports and a covert visit they apparently conducted recently, our operations are back on par with other hospitals in the region, and we are out of danger."

This was absolutely cause for celebration. Ravi immediately sent a warm message about the good news to all members of the leadership team, and invited them all to an after-hour celebration at a local bar. We had achieved our goal in less than sixty-five days! Clearly, we now had evidence that changing individual and team behavior was directly proportionate to changing organizational performance.

That evening, we met at the local bar and had a great time. We shared drinks, jokes, stories, and bonded as a leadership team. Everyone on Ravi's team was there, except of course, Janet Knutson.

The next morning, I stopped over at Janet's office, intent on learning more about her repeated absences at our LeaderPractice meetings.

"Janet, is everything okay? I asked. "You have missed practically all of our most important meetings."

"Everything's fine, Dr. Jordan."

"Can we talk candidly?" I asked.

"Certainly," she said, and I sat down.

"When I was at my last job," I said, in a calm, empathetic voice, "I was called to have a one-on-one leadership coaching session with one of the partners of our firm. She told me in no uncertain terms that I appeared very unhappy working there, and in hindsight, she was right. Eyes never lie, and I actually had tears in my eyes by the end of that conversation. I resigned after that discussion because these things are obvious to everyone. You can't lie about feelings because they will invariable show through your behavior. Everything seems to be improving around here, but from where I stand, it seems like something is not quite right with you. What exactly is going on?"

Janet shifted in her chair, as though there was a heavy weight on her shoulder. I hoped that she could tell I was there to help her, not to hurt her. At first, she avoided making direct eye contact with me, but then slowly, she collected herself, and in as clear a manner as I'd ever heard her speak, she calmly said the words I least expected to hear.

"Your consulting assignment with Middleville Hospital ends this week."

"What?" I stood up from my chair. What on earth was she talking about? Whose decision was it to end my assignment? As far as I could tell, I was hired by the board to serve as a leadership development consultant, and they had never said anything to me directly about a termination of my services.

"What are you talking about, Janet?"

"You heard me," she said. "It's over. Both you and Ravi will need to leave the organization by the end of this week."

"What brought this on?" I asked.

"It's nothing personal," she said. "The board has found a leadership solution for the hospital, so your assignment, as well as Ravi's interim CEO position is now at an end."

I stood up, shocked by her news. I collected my thoughts, and in a calm voice, I asked Janet Knutson the one question that was burning in my mind.

"Did they finally find a permanent CEO?"

"No."

"Then what leadership solution are you talking about?"

"The Board decided to give administrative authority to an existing leader in lieu of appointing or hiring a CEO."

"So, who is this new authority?"

"I am."

Part 3: The Greatness

Pelè Raymond Ugboajah, PhD

The Beginning

"It's called politics," Ravi said. "No amount of behavioral practice or team development can ever eradicate that particular organizational evil. It's just part of the human package."

Ravi and I were sitting at my dining room table, enjoying a delectable eggplant lunch dish a la Ruby's Trinidadian cooking style. Junior was lying happily on a mat by himself, studying the new world he was quickly growing into. At my request, Ruby finally stopped arranging, cooking, and preparing things, and came and sat for lunch at the table with Ravi and me. The world was at peace, but my heart was not. It had been several weeks since we left Middleville Hospital, and I still hadn't completely gotten over the sudden way in which Janet Knutson had discharged us.

"I guess for me, the real question is what's next with LeaderPractice," I said. "How will it make any money? We've shown that the model is successful, but in this small town, I really don't know where else to drum up any more business."

"Then give it away for free," Ravi said. "Remember, if you save one life, you save the world. That should be the goal—saving people's lives at work. In today's world, sometimes the best test of business value is if people will allow you to do something new for them for free. Once they fully buy into it, then you can start to think about monetization."

I thought about that for a moment. For most of my work life, I had struggled with organizational politics. I found myself wishing that someone could have introduced a process that would have given me a fighting chance to improve my own behaviors in a collaborative, safe, supportive environment like the one we were proposing through LeaderPractice. Maybe saving lives—like I wished mine had been saved—was the true purpose behind LeaderPractice, whether I knew it at the time or not.

Maybe the life I was saving … *was my own.*

I decided to ask Ravi the question that had been burning in my mind ever since we left the hospital. I had always wondered why he chose to stay in the small town of Middleville, even after his interim position expired.

"What about you, Ravi? What will you do next?"

"I'm doing it already."

"Doing what?"

"Following my bliss," he said, smiling. "As far as I can tell, I'm still the CEO of LeaderPractice, right?"

"Right!" I said, glowing with appreciation for the kind, gentle heart of the man. Suddenly, he started coughing uncontrollably. Ruby ran over to him and began checking to see what was wrong. As suddenly as he started, his cough stopped.

"My," he said, laughing, his face a little red. "I knew I loved hot, spicy food, but I didn't know it could give you chest pain!"

We weren't sure if we should laugh or be concerned. Ruby asked him if he had felt any such pains before. He brushed off the question in his usual, confident manner and complimented her on the food.

"This is really good stuff, Ruby!" he said. And he was right. Ruby could probably start a runaway, successful business cooking like that. She truly enjoyed cooking and was good at it. I was a lucky man in many ways.

Ruby cut into my thoughts as I was savoring her cooking. "Mike, why don't you and Ravi go over to Pastor Donahue's church and help him out there? Didn't he say he was having leadership issues as well?"

"Excellent idea!" I said, shaking my head and smiling at her.

"Cool beans!" she said. "That's why you keep me!"

We laughed.

"Ruby, that's a really good idea, though," Ravi said. "And what I like best about that idea is that it will be free and at a much different, smaller scale. We've shown that LeaderPractice works at a hospital, now, let's go make it work at a small church."

"Plus, they need a church band, Ravi. I think that's us," I said tongue-in-cheek.

"Absolutely!" he said, wolfing down Ruby's cooking. "That is most certainly us!"

Pelè Raymond Ugboajah, PhD

The Aftermath

We wasted no time calling Pastor Donahue after lunch. He was more than excited to have us conduct a discovery consultation at his church. We told him upfront and over the phone that our service would be free to him, and he was even more delighted. He asked us to come over that very same afternoon. Ravi and I drove together, and in less than five minutes, we pulled up to Pastor Donahue's Trinity Church.

"I've actually come to really appreciate this small-town lifestyle, Mike," Ravi said as I parallel parked in front of the church. "I'm hooked on the serenity, the slow driving, the trees, the lake—everything! I think the only thing I might want to skip is the cold midwestern winters I keep hearing about."

I agreed with him. "In the strangest way, I feel the same. I can't say I miss the hustle and bustle of Houston, LeaderTraits, or Enron much these days. Life is good."

"Yes," Ravi said, with a distant, hopeful look in his eyes. "Life is good."

Pastor Donahue literally jumped for joy when he saw us at his church door. He grabbed both Ravi and I and gave us his signature bear hugs. It was good to see the old geezer again.

"Boy," he said with his signature warmth on full display. "We really miss you guys at the hospital!" We sat down in his office while he handed out cans of pop.

"How is it going over there?" I asked.

"Well, things have really changed—and unfortunately—for the worse."

"How so?" Ravi asked.

"Well, I hate to ever say anything unpleasant about anyone, but Janet Knutson is a real donkey, if you know what I mean."

We chuckled. Good old Jake Donahue couldn't even bring himself to call someone an ass.

"We've always known that Janet was a piece of work, but now that they have given her administrative authority, she's totally out of control."

"Well, as they say," Ravi said. "Power corrupts, and absolute power corrupts absolutely."

"You betcha!" said Jake. "Janet Knutson behaves like a terrorist these days. Even though she's not the CEO, she figures the board is done trying to fill that position because no one will ever want to move up here permanently. So, she's reversed all the great new policies you guys put in place, especially the one about incentives for empathy and great team behavior. Now, nurses and doctors are back to their age-old antagonistic relationship with administrators, and they don't show up for shifts unless they absolutely have to. It looks like we're back to how things were before the RHC wrote us up the first time. Still no CEO, but even worse dysfunction than before!"

"Are you serious?" I asked. "Has it gotten that bad so fast?"

"Absolutely! Employee morale is down because of Janet's micromanaging style. Frankly, it's either been her way or the highway."

The Three Gaps between Goals and Greatness

"You know, I've always wondered," I said, "why was it that she was able to get rid of us so easily in the first place, even though we had achieved such great results?"

"Welcome to the real world!" Pastor Donahue laughed. "It's called cronyism. Janet goes way back with the leading and most influential members of the board. Heck, she's held powerful positions at Middleville Hospital for years now. This had less to do with you than with her growing level of influence at the board. She really didn't appreciate you guys because you did such a great job and made her look a little less like the kind of leader she wanted to portray. Basically, she knew she couldn't survive if you guys were around to watch her leadership style, so she surprised you first and got rid of you."

"Yeah," Ravi said. "Get rid of your enemies before they get rid of you. Excellent warfare strategy."

"Yes, and you know the first enemy she got rid of, right after you guys left?"

"Pat D'Arcy!" I said. "Anyone could have seen that one coming from a mile away. Poor Pat just doesn't know how to play organizational politics. She speaks her mind and is way too blunt and honest for her own good. Bless her heart! She's the classic 'good nurse, but…'"

"How are Amy and Elizabeth faring under Janet's administration?" Ravi asked.

"They are doing surprisingly well. Both of them got raises and were promoted to vice president positions, while I'm still languishing over there as a director, even though I've been there longer than both of them combined. But you know the worst part of this whole thing?"

"What could be worse?" I asked. We were definitely curious.

"I think Janet Knutson is doing something fishy."

"Like what?"

"Well, you know I run the purchasing department, and for some reason, she's been approving large purchases for furniture, a new car, and all kinds of things, while simultaneously endangering patients by not purchasing some of the critical equipment the hospital needs."

"What kind of equipment are we talking about?"

"A defibrillator console. She won't buy one. Our doctors have been saying we needed one of those for years, and now that we have some reimbursement coming in, we're all baffled as to why she won't get one."

"Is she trying to save money or something?" asked Ravi.

"That's been her standard excuse. She keeps saying we're a small town, and no one can expect us to have the best equipment. She says that's why we ship our toughest patients to nearby hospitals in bigger cities that can afford to buy those bigger pieces. To be perfectly honest, I think there is something unethical going on!"

Ravi and I looked at each other in silence. This wouldn't be the first unethical leader we'd come across. Janet Knutson was starting to sound more and more like some of the leaders we had interacted with at Enron.

"Okay, about your church," Ravi said, changing the subject. "What exactly do you see as the problem here?"

Pastor Donahue spent some time telling us what he knew about the situation. We advised him on some specific steps to take, including starting with some psychometric evaluations of his key people. We created a consulting plan and scheduled a LeaderPractice training session with his folks. He was delighted. He told us that if we can do even half of what we did at the hospital for his organization, he would be forever grateful.

On our way out, we ran into the twins, Emily and Dana Watson. They were just about to go in to visit Pastor Donahue to share their latest small-town chitchat.

"Howdy!" they announced in unison.

"Hello," I said. Ravi waved and said hello as well, and headed toward my car. The ladies didn't get the memo that we were leaving, and simply followed us to the car, chatting all the way.

"We're so sorry that you left the hospital!" Emily said. "We and most of the board members thought that you guys were doing such a great job!"

"Oh, thank you," I said, appreciating their kind words. Obviously, they and the others who liked us were not the more powerful members of the board, or the outcomes would have been different.

"I've always wondered," I asked, "How come it was so easy for Janet Knutson to get rid of us, even after we had essentially just saved the hospital from certain failure?"

"Oh, no," said Dana. "It wasn't really Janet Knutson that did you in at the board. Why, she's been trying to gain power for years. We all knew her tired old tricks."

"Then who was able to influence the board that way?" Asked Ravi, holding my car passenger door ajar, with one foot inside.

"It was Elizabeth Pierce and Amy Wells. They testified very negatively against you guys at the board and supported Janet's push to get you out."

Ravi and I looked at each other with expressions of shock on our faces. We never saw *that* coming.

Dana waved her hands across the sky as she explained further. "I just remember that look on Amy's face when she described you guys as big-city bounty hunters that weren't loyal to our small town. She said you would be gone immediately the next higher-paying consulting opportunity came along. I think the board voted to give administrative authority to Janet more out of frustration that no one will ever want to move up to our Middleville nowhere-land to fill the CEO spot. Janet certainly has no experience as a leader at that level, so I think the Board just gave in out of desperation."

We thanked Emily and Dana for their enlightening conversation and got into the car. Frankly, I was very upset, and in fact, I felt personally betrayed by Amy. Elizabeth was not a surprise to me, and I could care less because she had always presented herself as a wily, aloof, self-focused sycophant. Amy, on the other hand, had been a trusted confidant, and I had no idea that she would be singing for the highest bidder. Now I could see how and why they got their recent promotions! But then again, maybe this was their normal pattern. Amy had already once thrown Janet Knutson under the bus, so I guess it was to be expected that she would betray me someday as well. It is betrayal from those whom you grow to trust that truly hurts the most. I was disgusted with this latest revelation.

On the way back to my house, Ravi said, "Don't let this bother you, Mike. This is nothing new. All organizations are rife with politics. There is no panacea. People backbite, backstab, and gossip against each other all the time. What we need to do now is just focus on building LeaderPractice to become the kind of consulting firm that we envision. Let's focus on giving, not getting. Let's use our principles to help build environments where people can work in trust and openness."

I flashed a quick glance at Ravi as he spoke and realized just how much he had changed from the fast-talking, go-getting CEO of our former Enron-affiliated company, LeaderTraits. Now, the man sitting next to me was almost born anew. He seemed more like the wise father figure I never had, the great teacher, the enlightened soul who was seeking truth and oneness with the universe. Right then and there, Ravi walked on water as far as I was concerned. I was proud to work for him at our new firm, LeaderPractice.

"Thanks, Ravi."

"You betcha."

The Three Gaps between Goals and Greatness

Dinner With Ruby

I raised my glass to Ruby. "Here's to a new beginning," I said. She nodded, took a swig of her orange juice, and I took a first sip of my red merlot. Ruby refused to drink any alcohol, which was surprising because merlot was her favorite. We were just getting started with our family summit at Flying Deer, Middleville's only other high-end restaurant besides Big Bear. A year had not yet passed since our last summit, but so many things had already happened in our lives that we felt it was appropriate to sit down and do a systems check of how far we had come. It was evening, and a lonely sun was quickly vanishing behind the clouds above Middleville.

"So, what's good, and what's bad?" I asked.

"No, you go first," said Ruby.

"But I always go first—" I began to say, but she flashed me a firm look, and I gave in.

"Okay. What's good for me is that I am thrilled! Despite our abrupt exit from the hospital, Ravi has decided to stick it out with me while we work on what's next with our LeaderPractice business."

"That's really nice of him," Ruby said.

"Absolutely, and another thing is happening—I am writing a new song called 'She's a Good Nurse, But...' and Ravi has agreed to play guitar on it. I'm going to see if we can't work it into

LeaderPractice as a kind of theme song, so that whenever we're doing seminars, I can use it to segue into my musical instrument examples about the importance of practice in human behavior."

"This is really wonderful, honey," Ruby said. "It sounds like you're finally following your bliss!"

"Actually, I really am. I'm feeling really passionate and centered in this wonderful frame of mind where I know exactly why I'm doing LeaderPractice in the first place."

"And why are you doing it?" she asked.

"Because I think I've really been emotionally abused in organizations. It just seems like every job I've ever had has been full of painful, unfair politics. I find myself quitting often, afraid to be fired, afraid to feel the pain of not being in control of my own income, and potentially out of a job at any moment. I just couldn't handle everyone scrambling for power and willing to stomp everyone else out, using whatever political tricks they could. With all of my personal, behavioral failings, I just couldn't make it in that rat race. I envision a world in which organizations recognize that they really need to give their employees better tools to grow behaviors in safe environments. They really need to help people survive the onslaught of politics by collectively cultivating the right, supportive behaviors that will ultimately achieve their goals. Since I wasn't saved, I think LeaderPractice is my way to save other people's lives in organizations. If I can help organizations tame the behavior wars —the survival of the fittest wars—maybe I would have made a real contribution to someone else's life."

"I'm really proud of you, honey!"

"Thanks!" I really meant that. Ruby did not throw compliments out too readily, so I cherished anything that came from her.

"So, what's bad?" She asked.

"I guess the only thing that might not be so great is that we're going to have to make a decision pretty soon here. When Ravi and I begin searching for paying customers out of town, I will most likely have to be away from you and Junior for long periods of time. Unless we can grow the business 100% on the Internet, we might have to make a decision one way or another about how long we're going to live in Middleville."

"I knew you were going to say that," Ruby said. "So let me tell you this—whither thou goest, I will go!"

"Thanks, honey!" I said. "Now, what about you? What's good, and what's bad?"

"Well, what's good is that I love my life here in Middleville. I feel like good friends and people who appreciate me are everywhere. Actually, I feel like I have *family* here!"

"That's great," I said. "But how about your old feelings of failure? It seems to me like that is now a distant memory. Do you still feel like you're not the blazing success you envisioned in medical school?"

"Actually, I am still scared. Every single day when I answer the call and rush in, I am afraid of what I will meet, even though I put on my professional face. These people are not just patients to me—they're friends, real people with whom I've shared many years and both good times and bad times. I still have to brace myself when someone I know comes in with a terminal situation, and I just have to put my doctor face on everyday, and be strong."

Ruby was in tears, but I think these were tears of joy. One way or another, there *had* to be tears at our summits. I held her close and waited for the sobbing to end.

"So, what's bad?" I asked. She wiped her face.

"Actually, nothings is bad for me this time. It's really all good. But I have a little announcement to make."

"Uh oh!" I said. "Go ahead, what's the four-one-one?"

"We're pregnant!"

I looked around in the dark restaurant to see if it was appropriate for me to shout out in joy. It wasn't. There were too many people around. We were pregnant! What wonderful, powerful, life-making news! I motioned for the waiter to stop by and I ordered a full bottle of merlot. I was about to ask Ruby if she'd share it with me, and then, as she shook her head, I suddenly realized why she had refused the first glass of merlot in the first place. We toasted again, and this time … to life.

As we headed out of the restaurant, the phone rang. It was for Ruby, from the hospital. She nodded, said she'd be right there, and hung up the phone.

"Drive!" she practically shouted.

"What's going on?" I said. There are no doctors around, and they need me to come in. There has been an emergency!"

Without further ado, I put the pedal to the metal and drove. I think I must have very quickly exceeded the Middleville limit of thirty miles per hour.

The Emergency

I took Ruby straight to the hospital. She would not allow me to first take her home to get her things. We pulled up to the hospital to find police cars and an ambulance with their lights blazing, disrupting the otherwise peaceful Middleville night sky. You could hear police two-way radios buzzing along, providing orders and directions as they conducted their police business. Something significant was happening here.

Ruby motioned for me to leave. I thanked her for the wonderful news about the pregnancy, even as she was racing into the hospital. I drove back home, and considered if I ought to go and pick up Junior, whom we had left to spend the night at the home of one of Ruby's friends. I called over there and asked how the baby was doing. They said he was fast asleep, and so I decided to just go ahead and let him spend the night there. Besides, this would give me some time to put some finishing touches to my new song, "She's a Good Nurse, But…" As I drove home, I started running a melody and conceptual words through my head:

She's a good nurse, but…
Her behavior is so bad, making' everything thing so sad!
She's a good nurse, but…
Good behavior is the key, to effectivity!

Just before I pulled into our driveway, my phone rang. It was a nurse from the hospital.

"Dr. Mike Jordan?" she said, very formally. She must have been a new nurse who didn't know me personally.

"Speaking," I said.

"A patient has requested that you come to the hospital emergency room immediately. He is refusing emergency care and medication until he sees you and talks with you."

"I'll be right there," I said, turning my car around with a speed that surprised me. "Can you tell me the patient's name?" I asked.

"Yes," the nurse said. "Ravi Sharma."

I raced over to the hospital. My mind was an incoherent blur. I didn't know what to think. Ravi? Sick? Was *he* the emergency patient? I arrived at the hospital and raced into the emergency room. My worst fears were confirmed. There, on a bed in the emergency room floor, stuck full of wires and tubes, was my friend and mentor, Ravi Sharma.

I ran up to Ravi's bedside and motioned for some privacy. The nurse left the room. Ruby walked in.

"My good friend, Mike!" Ravi whispered; his eyes fixed on the ceiling.

"Honey, what on earth happened?" I asked Ruby.

"Ravi identified you as a friend in lieu of a next of kin, so we are able to share his medical information with you." Ruby was in doctor mode, steely, professional, and precise. The uninformed observer would never guess that she was my wife.

"So, what happened to him?" I asked again.

"He went into cardiac arrest, but we were able to revive him. We need to intubate him prior to safely transferring him to another hospital, but he refused anything that would put him into an unconscious state until he spoke with you. That's why you had to come in."

"Ravi," I said, turning to him. I had to lean close to his ear because his eyes were closed. He was breathing shallowly, with difficulty, and I wasn't sure if he could hear me.

"Keep talking to him," Ruby said, hurrying out to get prepared for her emergency intubation process.

"Ravi, I'm here," I said.

"Good," he said, managing a weak version of his signature rueful grin. "I need to tell you something very important."

"I'm here, Ravi," I said. "Tell me, so that they can take care of you!"

"I need you to promise me three things."

"Yes," I whispered. "Anything, Ravi."

"First, follow your bliss," he said. "Second, finish that new song of yours, and third…"

I couldn't hear him any more. I flashed Ruby a look of helplessness. Suddenly, another weak, faint whisper came out of his mouth.

"Save one life…"

He starting slipping in and out of consciousness, and managed to motion to one of the nurses. She understood his nonverbal request and screamed for Dr. Ruby Jordan. Ruby ran in, and asked me to leave. I did, and tears welled up in my eyes as I walked away, watching my wife and three nurses huddled over the struggling, physical body of my friend, Ravi Sharma.

I went home, threw myself in my favorite armchair, and sat there for hours, listening to the sounds of silence.

Pelè Raymond Ugboajah, PhD

When It Rains

The next morning, a very tired Ruby walked into our home. I had picked up Junior very early and had prepared some breakfast for her, knowing she'd be exhausted from the events of the night before. Since I was identified by Ravi as someone who should know his medical condition, I felt that I had a right to know what had transpired after I left.

"What happened?" I asked, as Ruby sat down on the living room floor, holding Junior extremely close.

"He was stabilized, but we had to fly him out to the nearest big city hospital."

"Was that because his condition was just too bad?"

"Not really. It was more because we just didn't have the right equipment. There is a limit to how far we can stretch this frontier medicine stuff."

I could tell that a part of Ruby was still in doctor mode. My wife wasn't yet fully home. "Will he be all right?"

"I don't know," she said. "For now, he's stable, but everything depends on what happens at the other hospital. We didn't have a defibrillator, so we had to use some really primitive methods to get his heart beating before the helicopter arrived."

"Thank goodness he's okay," I said. "I remember when he was sick the other day, and he complained of chest pain. And then it happened again at our house! I just didn't think to tell you, I could have let you know it had happened before…"

"It's no one's fault, Mike. Don't go there," Ruby said. "Despite our lack of equipment at the hospital, we did the best we could. Now we just have to hope for the best."

I turned on the TV. Sure enough, the local morning news was on, and the report from this event was already making its rounds.

"A former interim CEO of Middleville Hospital is in critical condition at La Crosse Hospital following a cardiac arrest. Reports indicate that a lack of defibrillator equipment at the originating hospital made his original care difficult. However, after heroic work from Middleville Hospital medical personnel, he was safely transported to La Crosse. We will update you as soon as we learn more about his condition."

I muted the TV volume. We sat speechless for almost an hour. Suddenly, the phone rang. It was Pastor Donahue.

"Mike," he said. "You won't believe what is going on right now."

"Try me," I said.

"Ravi's at La Crosse Hospital!"

"Unfortunately, I know that already. I was at Middleville Hospital with him last night."

"Well, here's something you probably don't know," he said.

"What?"

"Janet Knutson has been arrested!"

"Arrested?" I yelled out in a high squeal.

"Yes!" Jake Donahue said. "It's on TV right now! There was a covert operation put in place by the RHC after rumors were spreading about how bad her administrative decisions were. Apparently, through that process, the board found enough evidence to charge her with misappropriating funds."

"Wow." I said, noticing some breaking news come across on the TV screen. "I gotta go."

The Three Gaps between Goals and Greatness

I hung up the phone. *When it rains, it pours.* I was already in shock over the plight of our good friend, Ravi, and now this. I turned the TV volume back on, just in time to catch the latest incoming news.

"H.R. director Janet Knutson has been arrested," said a reporter, standing in front of Middleville City Hall. The TV camera panned from a view of the reporter to a view of Janet Knutson, in handcuffs, being led off into the courthouse. A crowd of townspeople watched as news crews stuck their microphones into her face, just in time for her to speak.

"I am innocent," she said, with composure and rehearsed poise. "I am confident that when things calm down, and we aren't so emotional about all this, I will be proven innocent."

Her lawyers whisked her away, and she disappeared into the crowd. Suddenly, I felt a sense of déjà vu. It occurred to me that I had seen that very same scene before on TV. The only difference was that the person who played Janet Knutson's role was a man— the CEO of Enron.

My palms began to sweat. I quickly thumbed through the cable channels again, frantically searching for more news. Ruby had her mouth open, equally in shock at the morning's various developments. *Yes, when it rains, it pours.* I finally found another local news station, and they were just announcing some more breaking news.

"This just in. Former Middleville Hospital interim CEO Ravi Sharma has just been pronounced dead. La Crosse Medical Center doctors were unable to save him…"

Pelè Raymond Ugboajah, PhD

Following Bliss

I was numb. I felt nothing. It was the day after, and ever since the very early morning hours, I had been sitting and staring out of our bedroom window, watching the day begin and thinking of my friend and mentor, Ravi Sharma. Ruby had to go to work, and she took Junior to day care. Instinctively, twice I almost picked up the phone to call Ravi's cell phone, to tell him something, or to seek his wisdom and advice; twice I pulled back, remembering that Ravi was no longer with us. *Ravi was gone!* He had followed his bliss to its ultimate conclusion. The tears had flowed so freely all morning that I had none left. I just sat there in our room feeling empty, lonely, and afraid.

The telephone rang, saving me from my own thoughts.

"Mike?" It was Pat D'Arcy. "My deepest condolences, Mike!"

"Thanks, Pat," I said. "I meant to call you ever since I learned about your termination at the hospital."

"Oh, that's no big deal," she said. "Janet got what was coming to her. Have you read the newspaper today?"

"No," I said.

"Well, you might want to. Your wife is on the front page!"

I ran out to our mailbox and grabbed a copy of the *Middleville Star*. Sure enough, right there on the front page was a picture of

Ruby in her full doctoral regalia, with several nurses standing by her side. The caption read:

HEROES!

The article explained how Dr. Ruby Jordan and her medical team had initially saved former CEO Sharma's life. Even though he died at La Crosse Hospital a day later, the article went on to explain that the Doctors at La Crosse were surprised that he had even made it to their hospital. All indications were that the Middleville medical team's heroic actions extended his life for at least a day because of their quick thinking and frontier medicine, despite their lack of some critical medical technology.

The article continued by explaining that former H.R. director Janet Knutson, who had just been fired by the board of trustees, had successfully posted bail and vowed to fight legal accusations that her policies and alleged misappropriation of funds were to blame for the death of former interim CEO Ravi Sharma.

The phone rang. I put the paper down and picked up the receiver. It was Amy Wells.

"Mike," she said. "I'm so sorry!"

"That's okay, Amy."

"I need to apologize to you about my testimony to the board. I was just doing what I felt I needed to do to stay alive in our organization. I admit it was terrible, betraying behavior."

I sat silent for a moment. In my mind, I was replaying Ravi's advice to me: *save one life.* No matter how bitter I felt toward her, I knew I had to put my pain away.

"Amy, all is forgiven and forgotten," I said. "We all need a safe place to practice those negative behavioral tendencies away. That's what LeaderPractice is for. Let me know if I can ever be of help to you."

I said good-bye and hung up the phone, albeit rather abruptly. I stared blankly at the handset for a few minutes, and it rang again. It was Amy again.

"Is there anything I can do to help you?" she asked, her voice loaded with regret. "Maybe I could put in a good word so the board can hire you back. You know we now have both the CEO and H.R. leadership positions open."

Clearly she was suffering from the guilt of having betrayed Ravi and me.

"No," I said, "but thanks for asking."

"So, what will you do next?" she asked.

"I think I'll just follow my bliss." I said.

Pelè Raymond Ugboajah, PhD

Save One Life

Eight months passed by very quickly. LeaderPractice had acquired some new clients in the surrounding midwestern states, and I had become extremely busy doing the speaker circuits to promote our business. As a result of an aggressive Internet marketing strategy, we were growing rapidly. In addition to restarting the LeaderPractice methodology at Middleville Hospital, we were quickly becoming a household name whenever organizations thought about the concept of leadership practice. Pastor Jake Donahue resigned from the hospital, and he and Pat D'Arcy joined me to help run the business. Our organizational motto was Ravi's last words—Save One Life—and we were proud of the passionate calling we shared to create safe leadership development environments in organizations of all sizes. Working with Jake and Pat was simply amazing. We shared honesty, camaraderie, openness, and a common vision. The honesty and trust in our growing team was refreshing, and we were proud that our firm, LeaderPractice, Inc., was practicing what it preached.

A very pregnant Ruby and I still had a few important questions to answer. Would we stay in Middleville? Would LeaderPractice have to be headquartered in a big city? Would Ruby ever return to finish her residency, or would she focus on raising our kids? We decided to just let time answer these questions for us.

We were settling down to dinner one evening when the doorbell rang. It was Emily and Dana Watson.

"Hello, Dr. Ruby!" Emily sang.

Ruby let them in. They had never visited our home before, so I was extremely curious. I hoped nothing was wrong at the hospital. We completed a round of chitchat, and then Emily and Dana got down to why they came.

"Dr. Jordan," said Emily, looking me squarely in the face. "There's a murmur in the community that you'd be a great fit for the CEO position at Middleville Hospital."

I looked at Ruby with an incredulous look on my face. I had never heard about this. This was certainly news to me.

"I haven't heard this murmur," I said, humoring her. "Tell me all about it."

"Well," said Dana, taking over from her sister. "We hear things on the board, you know, and people are wondering how it might be if you interviewed for the job. There's a strong chance you might be selected for the position if you did."

"Wouldn't you be interested in someday actually becoming a CEO?" Emily asked, jumping back into the conversation.

I looked at Ruby, almost as though I needed her permission. She said nothing but nudged me onward with her eyes. LeaderPractice was doing so well now. I had finally found a calling that I was passionate about; something I truly felt was making a contribution to organizations. I couldn't leave that now, no matter how much status and financial promise came with a CEO position. I had to be honest with them.

"Emily and Dana. Thank you so much for this news," I said. "The truth is, I'm really flattered. But here's the problem."

"What?" they said in unison, with expectation on their faces.

"I've finally found a purpose in my life. The work we do here at LeaderPractice is literally saving people's work lives. I've got to follow this thing to its logical conclusion."

"Here, Emily," Dana said, playfully motioning to Emily. "Let me help you with that big foot in your mouth!"

We laughed a little bit over that, and sat back and enjoyed their company while they recited for us all the little secrets they could muster up about everyone in town. They also told us that the LeaderPractice process we had helped to restart at the hospital had proven to be exactly what they needed to improve leadership and employee morale. Later on, Ruby insisted that I play my new song —'She's a Good Nurse, But...'—on our living room baby grand piano. About an hour later, the twins got up to leave.

"Dr. Ruby," Emily said as she was putting on her coat, "Do you know if it's a boy or a girl?"

"I didn't want to know," she said, "but Mr. LeaderPractice over here insisted."

"So what is it?" Dana asked, almost jumping up and down in excitement.

"It's a boy," I said.

"Ooh!" Emily gushed. "Another one to pass your family business to, huh?"

"Yeah," I said. "The way he kicks around in there, I wouldn't be surprised if he becomes the CEO someday!"

Dana jumped in, not to be outdone by her sister. "Have you guys picked out a name yet?"

"Yes," I said, with pride. "His name is Ravi."

Pelè Raymond Ugboajah, PhD

THE POINT

Pelè Raymond Ugboajah, PhD

People Issues

An ostrich with its head in the sand is just as blind to opportunity as to disaster. —Anonymous

In the global race to achieve faster, better, cheaper business greatness, most leaders face a huge gap between the goals they set and the actual results achieved by the people in their organizations. This phenomenon does not show a failure to plan, but rather, a failure to *execute*. In an article for the *Harvard Business Review*, researchers Mankins and Steele found that this execution gap can be responsible for a nearly 40% loss in an organization's financial value. According to other studies by Norton & Kaplan, Bersin & Associates, and the Corporate Strategy Board, here are some of the main reasons why the execution gap exists:

- 95% of the workforce doesn't understand company goals

- 86% of the workforce is not motivated

- 84% of companies aren't maximizing workforce potential

- 50% of the average workforce's capacity is wasted

Given these bleak findings, how can companies reliably bridge the gap between their goals and their desired greatness? What exactly is the *nature* of this gap? While there are many possible explanations for the root cause of the gap, the one common, recurring element is a stubborn, nagging blind spot:

People issues.

Pelè Raymond Ugboajah, PhD

They won't go away. They are always around. No matter how much you try to avoid them by setting goals and staying busy, people issues are always right in front of you, either helping or hurting your organization's competitive advantage in the marketplace.

I once served in an organization that was experiencing extreme dysfunction and a huge execution gap at all levels of the company. The CEO invited the executive leadership team to an off-site managerial retreat, where we discussed the challenges we were facing in the context of some well-known management books. During that retreat, we all agreed that, according to the concepts in those books, our organization was most dysfunctional in the area of people issues. We also agreed that we needed to follow the three-, five-, or twelve-step programs that were scattered throughout these volumes to close the execution gap we were facing. However, once we got back to our offices, there was no follow-up or execution of the agreed strategies and goals. Collectively, we buried our heads in work, and despite my constant reminders to the team, no one could find the time to address those people issues on a daily basis. By the time we met at the next management retreat, the organizational dysfunction and execution gap had worsened.

By ignoring people issues, we were acting like ostriches.

Just as an ostrich can't get away from a charging lion by burying its head in the sand, one cannot get away from the impact of interpersonal behavioral issues by burying oneself in work.

The Three Gaps between Goals and Greatness

> Demanding better performance from people does not bridge the business execution gap. The solution lies in creating lasting behavioral change in people, which will in turn produce better performance.

Pelè Raymond Ugboajah, PhD

The Three Gaps

Character is higher than intellect. —Ralph Waldo Emerson

Organizations don't become great because they set great goals. They become great because *great* leadership is in place to inspire and motivate people to get great things done. Every year, companies spend millions on a variety of training efforts and performance management initiatives aimed at trying to close the execution gap between goals and greatness. Unfortunately, these programs find little or no success because they are focusing on the wrong set of challenges. The real challenge is to truly understand the nature of the business execution gap and to recognize that it is not one monolithic performance gap. The execution gap between goals and greatness is actually comprised of three people-related gaps:

GAP 1: Behavior

The first gap is a lack of focus on organizational behavior. Most organizations focus far too much time and resources on performance goals and outcomes, while simultaneously allowing behavior to evolve in a Darwinian, political free-market environment where those who survive are usually the wiliest politicians. Indeed, performance goals can be tangibly measured and monitored, but they are influenced greatly by the softer side of business—human behavior, which is much harder to measure, manage, and monitor. The organization that is able to focus on leadership and employee behavior by assessing, monitoring, and nurturing it, will see exponentially improved performance results.

GAP 2: Habits

The second gap occurs when organizations don't create opportunities for their people to turn desired behavioral skills into habits. It is not enough to know what to do. You have to actually do what you know, do it well, and do it repeatedly until it becomes second nature. For example, most people are aware of (and agree with) the principles Stephen Covey laid out in *The Seven Habits of Highly Effective People*. But how many people have actually made the time to practice those seven identified behaviors until they become habits? Yet any great athlete, artist, or musical performer will tell you that they rely faithfully on the old adage: *practice makes perfect*. The organization that is committed to carving out some time to help its leaders grow positive behavioral and leadership habits will see a solid increase in employee performance.

GAP 3: Community

The third gap occurs when organizations do not form safe communities of practice where their people can practice positive behavioral habits together. Leadership development results can be significantly improved when individual practice is augmented with the active participation and feedback of others. Human beings are social by nature and are thus able to achieve much more with the trust, positive conflict, feedback, recognition, mentorship, and accountability that are inherent to communities of practice. A community built around the collective goal of improving leadership behavior can help to increase one's chances of new-skill development in the same way a Toastmasters club or a Weightwatchers group can for their members.

How to Close the Three Gaps

The key to successful leadership today is influence, not authority.
—*Kenneth Blanchard*

T he three gaps between goals and greatness manifest in organizations as a pervasive leadership gap. Without great leadership, organizations will be mired in team dysfunction, lack of productivity, and overall inefficiency. For the best clues on how to close these 'execution gaps', one must examine the following opportunities and threats in today's leadership landscape:

- Only Great Leadership Can Close the Execution Gap

- There Is a Growing Shortage of Great Leaders

- Most Leaders Don't Focus on the Goose

- There Can Be No Lasting Change Without Practice

Only Great Leadership Can Close the Execution Gap:
Nothing affects the success of an organization more than the quality of its leadership. Not strategy, not technology, not systems, not innovation, and not processes. The single most important factor for bridging the business execution gap is people, and the only way to reliably and predictably improve the effectiveness and productivity of people is through great leadership at all levels of an organization.

There Is a Growing Shortage of Great Leaders:
The demographic reality of our time suggests that there is a shortage of great leaders in most organizations. Additionally, those baby-boom leaders are fast approaching retirement, but there aren't

new leaders ready and prepared to fill their spots in the leadership pipeline. General Electric, one of the most celebrated organizations of our era, was successful not only because of one great leader, Jack Welch, but also because of the many leaders he developed in the company's leadership pipeline. In order to become truly great, organizations must implement cultures and systems that continuously develop new leaders to replace the retiring generation.

Most Leaders Don't Focus on the Goose

While most leaders work hard to create high-performance in their firms (the golden egg), they don't usually assign the same level of importance and attention to employee behavior (the goose). In Aesop's parable, The Goose and the Golden Eggs, an intense desire to acquire more golden eggs led a greedy owner to kill the goose. By focusing so intensely on the golden eggs at the expense of the goose, he ended up losing both and having none. This parable makes a simple, self-evident point: You must take care of not only that which you seek, but also, that which produces what you seek. In order to increase organizational success, companies must focus on improving the behavior of their leaders and employees, because that is what will in turn improve company-wide performance.

There Can Be No Lasting Change without Practice:

Here's a little-known fact: many efforts to develop leaders do not succeed. Another little-known fact: a 10:20:70 rule states that traditional classroom training, which is at the core of most of these efforts, is only 10% as effective as two other elements in the learning mix: mentoring (20%) and practice (70%). By focusing so much on traditional training and the occasional mentoring efforts, organizations are missing out on the most powerful method available for actually implementing lasting behavioral change—*practice!* Great athletes, musicians, or public speakers know the value

The Three Gaps between Goals and Greatness

of consistent practice, and any neuroscientist will tell you that the mind learns best through experience and repetition.

Pelè Raymond Ugboajah, PhD

The Solution Is Practice!

We are what we repeatedly do. Excellence, therefore, is not an act, but a habit. —Aristotle

L eaderPractice is a leadership development process and software solution that helps organizations bridge the gap between goals and greatness. With LeaderPractice, desired organizational behaviors are practiced in the safety of a community environment until they become habits.

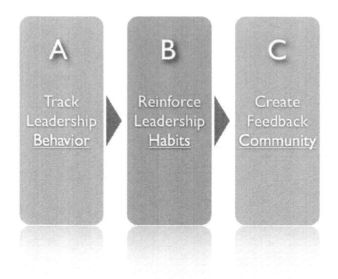

The driving concept behind LeaderPractice comes from the 'ABC' principles of behavioral psychology—antecedents, behaviors, and consequences—which show that a person's likelihood of developing

The Three Gaps between Goals and Greatness

a behavior is dependent on the reinforcement received during the practice of that particular behavior.

The LeaderPractice solution focuses attention on the three 'people' gaps between goals and greatness:

The Gap	LeaderPractice Solution
Behavior	Identify and focus on developing leadership behavior that will close the execution gap.
Habits	Practice leadership behaviors in an action-learning context until they become habits.
Community	Cohorts provide each other with feedback and positive reinforcement.

Practicing leadership behavior is not very different from the way in which any other human skills are developed. For example, consider what it takes to practice a piano. It turns out that the learning process for becoming great at piano playing is essentially the same as what you'd find for becoming a great leader. The difference is in the context and details, but not the main learning process itself. LeaderPractice simply provides a social software environment where that practice can be positively reinforced, rewarded, shaped, measured, and monitored.

Following is a high-level comparison of the habit-forming process on a piano to the same process when it comes to practicing and

Pelè Raymond Ugboajah, PhD

developing leadership behaviors:

Step	Piano Practice	Behavior Practice
1.	Learn a new piano phrase	Learn a new leadership behavior, model, or skill
2.	Divide the phrase into left and right hand parts	Divide the new skill into its constituent model parts
3.	Reduce tempo	Reduce risk through role-play with fewer, trusted partners away from real work situations
4.	Repeat until new habits form	Repeat until new habits form
5.	Assemble left and right hands and repeat until combined habits form	Assemble model parts and repeat until habits form
6.	Perform at the right tempo, and in real situations	Perform in the workplace, in real situations

Just as you can schedule lessons to learn the piano, you can also schedule LeaderPractice in your workplace. And you can start implementing some of these practices right now!

Identify Behavioral Results, Reasons, and Rewards:
Each leadership participant will begin the process by providing a vision statement that describes the personal reasons, sense of urgency, and motivation regarding why they will fully invest and remain engaged in the ongoing weekly leadership practice process. Each participant's behavioral goals are tracked on a weekly basis, and uploaded to an enterprise-wide performance-management

software system. In such an enterprise information system, behavioral goals can be viewed, shared, and collaboratively managed, alongside the more tangible performance goals. At the end of the year, rewards are attached to agreed levels of behavioral achievement, alongside the rewards that are normally provided for achieving performance goals.

Define Unique Leadership Competencies:

Now it is time to identify the core, unique leadership qualities that will propel the organization to competitive advantage and differentiation in its business landscape. For one organization it could be leadership qualities such as strategic thinking or coaching, and for another, it could be innovation. Following this identification, a leadership success profile must be developed that states these leadership competencies while outlining the specific behaviors, habits, knowledge, roles, and skills that make those qualities possible.

Select and Assess Leadership Participants:

Once the target leadership behavioral competencies and goals are identified at the organizational level, individual leaders from each management level of the organization need to be selected and assessed using inputs from multiple sources (such as psychometric personality tests, multirater/360-degree tools, and leadership interviews). The result of this assessment process is an *Ostrich Card*, which is either a physical card or a software application that highlights the top three strengths and destructive behaviors of each participant, (including suggestions for how to address them in real time or in stressful situations). The leader would carry the ostrich card at all times (i.e., in order to keep his or her head out of the sand).

228

Pelè Raymond Ugboajah, PhD

Following is an example of some of the strengths and weaknesses that might be identified on an ostrich card:

OSTRICH CARD		
STRENGTHS	DERAILERS	SUGGESTIONS
Empathetic	Self-Important	
Optimistic	Pessimistic	
Forthcoming	Uncommunicative	
Delegating	Micromanaging	
Dependable	Unpredictable	
Courageous	Overly-Nice	
Respectful	Sycophant	
Amicable	Combative	
Trusting	Detached	
Truthfulness	Ambiguous	

Align Behavior and Performance to Organizational Goals
Once leaders are identified and assessed, it is time to align behavioral goals with performance goals, which must in turn be aligned to the very highest goals of the organization. Like a pyramid, every behavioral and performance goal must be linked to the overall goals and vision of the organization.

Practice, Measure, and Monitor Behavior Goals
Measurement criteria should be assigned to every behavioral and performance goal and monitored in a software tool on a computer or a Smartphone. The software tool allows the participant to self-record weekly behavior observations and generates a graphic dashboard of behavioral progress for collaborative discussions with others.

Hold Weekly LeaderPractice Meetings

The Three Gaps between Goals and Greatness

The participants in the leadership development process will meet weekly to leverage the power of communities of practice. Each meeting is held for an hour at least once a week. Each meeting provides an opportunity for each of the three gaps −(behavior, habits, and community) to be closed. Each meeting will include three sections:

(a)Impromptu simulations, role-plays, and games
(b)Prepared 'teachable moment' speech
(c)Participant feedback and evaluations.

Use a Trained Facilitator and Project Manual
LeaderPractice meeting participants will work together in accordance with a LeaderPractice project manual that outlines twelve carefully scripted leadership simulations, role-plays, games, and the overall LeaderPractice meeting practice process itself. Each of these projects addresses a core leadership behavioral competency. A trained facilitator is assigned to each LeaderPractice meeting to ensure adherence to the manual and to record the results of the overall meeting process.

Pelè Raymond Ugboajah, PhD

LeaderPractice

We cannot solve our problems with the same thinking we used when we created them. —Albert Einstein

L eaderPractice is a decidedly different approach to leadership development, although it is based on proven, brain-based learning principles that will help increase productivity, reduce team dysfunction, and achieve organizational greatness. Here are three specific things you can do right now to begin closing the three gaps between goals and greatness at your organization:

1. **BEHAVIOR**: Get the FREE LeaderPractice Gap Assessment and request a Software Trial from www.resultpal.com. Normally valued at $500 USD, this assessment will give you a good idea of where you stand in terms of how people issues are helping or hindering your organizational greatness. Additionally, the ResultPal Software Trial will help leaders in your organization see behavior as something that should be measured, monitored, and managed at the same level of granularity as performance.

2. **HABITS**: Create 'action-learning' or 'on-the-job' opportunities for people to practice improving leadership strengths and reducing behavioral weaknesses.

3. **COMMUNITY**: Use ResultPal software to manage, monitor, and measure leadership development. By creating virtual (and physical) communities of practice, you will provide leaders

the kind of social feedback, encouragement, and
accountability that will greatly accelerate their development.

LeaderPractice helps companies improve productivity and
performance by developing great leaders at all levels of the
organization.

You can start this process today with a FREE LeaderPractice Gap
Assessment and Software Trial from ResultPal: For more
information, please visit www.resultpal.com.

Pelè Raymond Ugboajah, PhD

She's A Good Nurse, But...

I know a nurse at a hospital
She was definitely good, although never understood
She didn't know office politics
So she failed to get along, she was right and they were wrong
She walked, talked like she ran the place
Making everybody mad, micromanaging so bad
Now she's sad 'cause she lost her job
And she goes without a smile, a victim of her style

(Okay, so she's got a problem with people skills…)
She's a good nurse, but...
Her behavior is so bad, making everything so sad
She's a good nurse, but…
Good behavior is the key, to effectivity

Every little thing you do
Every little thing you say
Will get political reactions (at work)
So please practice people skills, if you want to pay the bills
You gotta know how to walk the talk
Taking everybody high, making everything alright
You need to get LeaderPractice
Turn your negativity into positivity

(Her technical skills are great, but her people skills?)
She's a good nurse, but...
Her behavior is so bad, making everything so sad
She's a good nurse, but…
Good behavior is the key, to effectivity

If practice makes perfect
You can polish up your act, close the execution gap
You need to get LeaderPractice
Turn your negativity into positivity

(Y'know, people really need LeaderPractice!)
She's a good nurse, but...

© 2011 LeaderPractice—written, produced, and performed by Pele R. Ugboajah, PhD.

About the Author

D r. Pelè Raymond Ugboajah is an author, speaker, coach, musician, and software developer. He is the founder of ResultPal: a practice-based performance, coaching, and engagement software tool for coaches and growing organizations.

Born and raised in a war-torn African refugee village, he was named after Pelè of Brazil—the greatest soccer player on earth—whose influence was so great that it stopped a bloody civil war. Pelè internalized his namesake's simple, yet powerful secret of success—*practice*—and later transformed it, developing his own unique skills in music, writing, and motivational speaking. Eventually, Pelè turned his attention to the world of business, where he created LeaderPractice—a signature process for helping organizations bridge the gaps between goals and greatness.

Pelè holds an MBA and a PhD specializing in leadership development. Over the years, he has authored several books, major label songs, and has spoken to diverse business audiences. In 2006, he became the Toastmasters District Six Champion of Public Speaking.

Prior to founding ResultPal, Pelè worked at Parametric Technology Corporation, Electronic Data Systems, MDA Leadership Consulting, and Rainy Lake Medical Center, where he was vice president of human resources.

For more information, please visit www.resultpal.com.

Pelè Raymond Ugboajah, PhD

4884555R00131

Made in the USA
Lexington, KY
14 January 2016